PRACTICAL MARKETING

D0546127

PRACTICAL MARKETING PLANNING

John Cooper
and
Peter Lane

MACMILLAN
Business

First published 1997 by
MACMILLAN PRESS LTD
Houndmills, Basingstoke, Hampshire RG21 6XS
and London
Companies and representatives
throughout the world

ISBN 0–333–67907–5
ISBN 0–333–67908–3

A catalogue record for this book is available
from the British Library.

10   9   8   7   6   5   4   3   2   1
06   05   04   03   02   01   00   99   98   97

Copy-edited and typeset by Povey–Edmondson
Tavistock and Rochdale, England

Printed in Great Britain by
Antony Rowe Ltd, Chippenham, Wiltshire

Contents

List of Figures

PART I
The Marketing Planning Process

CHAPTER 1

Marketing: What's It All About?

A traditional market square on market day is the natural beginning of the marketing process. Buyers meet sellers, and they trade. The best produce sells at good prices but poor produce is often left on the stall or has to be sold cheaply at the end of the day.

All over the world, for generations buyers and sellers have met face to face on the market square and bartered, argued, haggled and traded – they are natural marketers always in tune with the needs of their customers.

But then, as businesses all over the world became bigger and more organised, managers often lost that direct contact with their customers and as a result some companies, without realising what was happening, started to produce products that their customers didn't really want. Having lost touch they continued to develop and sell the products that they could make, rather than finding out what their customers really wanted and adapting their production to make those products.

> 'You can have your car in any colour you like, as long as it's black.'
> (Henry Ford)

They became production driven rather than consumer driven.

Part of the reason for the development of production orientation amongst UK producers stemmed from historical precedent. As the world's premier trading nation from the middle ages to the latter half of the nineteenth century, producers had the advantage of monopoly trading terms with the rapidly increasing number of newly discovered lands in the new worlds: the Americas, Africa, India and Australasia. Exports of various products to countries other than these were banned or controlled to protect the home market and imports were subject to prohibitively high rates of duty and other extreme penalties, as the extract from an Elizabethan statute illustrates (Figure 1.1).

Queen Elizabeth I
Award For Exporting
Without Permission

First time exporters
– forfeit all goods plus
1 year in prison plus
left hand off and nailed
up on market day

Second time exporters
– death

Figure 1.1   Elizabethan shield

The development of the industrial era from the middle of the eighteenth century onwards only helped to make matters worse. By being at the forefront of industrial development, the newly emerging British industrial companies sold everything they could make, often regardless of the needs of the consumer. For example in one year alone (1886) the steel producers of the West Midlands produced and exported over one thousand million steel pen nibs at a time when fewer than one million people in the world could write.

UK producers flourished by supplying captive overseas markets, firstly the colonies, then the Empire and latterly the Commonwealth. Because these markets and the home market were protected from imported goods, prices could be controlled, enabling production-orientated businesses to thrive throughout the nineteenth century and right up until the late 1970s (although there are still plenty of examples left today if you know where to look).

About thirty years ago, as consumers started to become more affluent they also started to become more selective, and began to demand a greater variety of goods and prices. During the 1960s and 1970s the abolition of retail price maintenance and decreasing import restrictions gave consumers the wider freedom of choice they wanted:

- They chose to listen to Japanese radios.
- They chose to drive German cars.

- They chose to eat French cheese.
- They chose to go on cheap Spanish holidays.
- **They chose not to buy British!**.

As a result huge sectors of industry collapsed because they couldn't adapt quickly enough. The directors and managers of these businesses had only been taught how to design and produce products and to manage factories and people. They just didn't know how to find out what people wanted!

> They didn't understand the concept of marketing or the marketing process.

Although in recent years many businesses have adopted the marketing concept and prospered as a result, a high percentage of these are retailers or service providers. Much of the UK manufacturing industry still appears to be production led and as consumers we still prefer to buy products from other countries. Even though a large number of foreign-owned businesses established factories in the UK during the 1980s and 1990s, the UK's visible balance of trade is still consistently £2–3 billion in deficit every quarter – that adds up to over £10 000 000 000 every year!

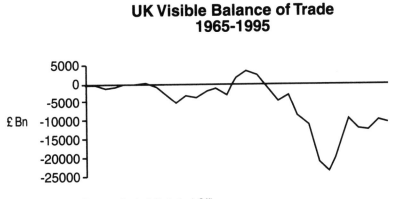

**UK Visible Balance of Trade
1965-1995**

Source: Central Statistical Office

Figure 1.2   **UK visible balance of trade**

> We still continue to buy more than we sell!

But even before the industrial revolution started a radical thinker called Adam Smith defined the marketing concept. In 1776 he wrote what has come to be regarded as one of the first economics textbooks: *An Inquiry into the Nature and Causes of the Wealth of Nations.*

In his summary on the mercantile system he concluded that: 'Consumption is the sole end and purpose of production; and the interest of the producer ought to be attended to only so far as it may be necessary for promoting that of the consumer. The maxim is so perfectly self-evident that it would be absurd to attempt to prove it'. This statement is still valid over two hundred years later and is still used today to describe the marketing concept.

In recent years the Chartered Institute of Marketing produced a more current definition of the marketing concept which is:

> 'Marketing is the management process *responsible for identifying, anticipating* and satisfying customer requirements . . . *profitably.'*

That last word is important because almost anybody providing a business or a service can satisfy the requirements of their customers, clients, patients or passengers if making a profit (or a profitable return on capital) is not an important consideration. For example:

- A health authority could provide operations upon demand as well as unlimited medical and nursing care.

- A local authority could provide all the services required by all the different sections of the population in its area.

- An engineering company could develop products of the highest possible quality.

And they all have at one time or another! You can probably think of plenty of examples:

- The NHS

- Numerous local authorities

- Companies such as Rolls-Royce

But all these institutions and organisations have learnt to their cost that there has to be a balance between the needs of the customer and those of the supplier.

The secret of good marketing is not just to identify and satisfy your customer's requirements but to satisfy them at a price that is acceptable to both of you – one that provides you with a profit and also ensures that the customer is retained as a future purchaser:

> customer satisfaction + supplier profitability = repeat sales

Unless you are a monopoly supplier, to achieve this balance you need to be market focused, continually aware of what your customers think and how your market is behaving.

■ A Market-Focused Business

As we have already mentioned, the secret of good marketing is not only to identify and satisfy your customer's requirements but also to try to develop customer loyalty, encourage repeat purchases and make a profit (or achieve a defined objective).

In a market-focused organisation everybody from the managing director right down to the most junior employee is constantly aware that without a continuous flow of satisfied customers that make repeat repurchases, the business would stagnate, job prospects would diminish and sooner or later jobs would disappear.

Getting your customer to like you, or at least to like doing business with you, is becoming increasingly vital to businesses of all types – transport, retail, financial services and so on – as usually it is all too easy for the customer to walk away and buy elsewhere.

> Getting your customer to like you means that you have to make an extra effort to find out what they want and then provide it – *at a profit*.

Market-focused businesses that have absorbed the marketing concept of concentrating on the needs of their customers will always do better in the long term than production-focused businesses because they do most or all of the following, which help to make them more competitive:

- They take notice of what people want.
- They observes changes in demand.

- They see opportunities before others.
- They are aware of competitor activity.
- They keep their customers informed.
- They know where the business is going and how much effort is required to get there.

A production or inwardly-focused business ignoring the above will lose out in a competitive market and lose customers.

How many disadvantages of not being a market-focused company can you list?

```
....................................................................
....................................................................
....................................................................
....................................................................
....................................................................
```

In a market-focused business two of the main roles of marketing are:

- Anticipating future trends and developing appropriate products and service.
- Helping to maintain current marketing activities and monitoring past performance.

Because of this diversity of activities a market-focused business needs to be able to work in a variety of time frames, for example:

- Gathering and analysing data from the past (sales, profit, costs and so on)
- Implementing and monitoring current activities (promotions, advertising).
- Customer care planning for the next season.
- Researching future market and customer trends.

All this at the same time!

It is worth mentioning at this point that to do these jobs properly marketing needs to have control over its own budget, otherwise there may be times when part of the budget is reallocated for a variety of reasons without considering the effect this may have on future marketing activities.

■ The Components of Marketing

Marketing consists of four component parts. The first three are the prime principles of marketing and the fourth is the collection of tools and techniques that help to translate marketing principles into measurable results. The four components are:

- **The concept of marketing**   This is the who? where? why? where? and how? of marketing. A clear understanding of the customer and the market place is the first principle of marketing, without this understanding nothing else works.

- **The marketing mix**   The marketing mix is a combination of all the elements that can affect the successful development of profitable business. Ensuring that the product, price, place, promotion etc. are just 'right' is the second principle of marketing.

- **The marketing planning process**   Plan, review, revise and replan is the third principle of marketing. Accepting the need for constant planning and regular reviews followed by plan revisions as objectives are gained or changed is a basic prerequisite for success in today's competitive market place.

- **The marketing tools**   The marketing tools are a range of techniques and activities that can be used to help a business plan and implement its strategy successfully.

■ The Marketing Concept

The first principle of marketing is the concept or philosophy of marketing. Accepting the concept of marketing and adopting a market focused approach to business, putting the needs of the customer first, are essential for all businesses – firstly to help ensure survival and secondly to help develop profitable growth. It is all about orientating the business towards its customers:

```
no customers = no business
```

■ The Marketing Mix

The marketing philosophy, once adopted by a business, can be seen in its marketing mix. The marketing mix is a combination of all the factors that can affect the successful development of a profitable business.

The emphasis placed on any of the elements of the marketing mix may change depending on the type of business, its market place and its strategic objectives. Once a business adopts the marketing concept, the marketing department becomes the pivotal centre of the business, helping to coordinate the elements of the mix and ensuring that everyone who contributes understands their involvement in helping the business to succeed.

The main constituents of the marketing mix are often known as 'The 7 Ps':

- Product
- Price
- Place
- Promotion
- Participants
- Presence
- Process

Figure 1.3 helps to illustrate the relationship between each of the main constituents.

Figure 1.3   The marketing mix

Each of the 7 Ps in turn has its own mix of constituents, and the degree of importance placed on any one component will vary from industry to industry and business to business.

- **The PRODUCT characteristics**   These attributes are the main characteristics of the product. Some or all of these may apply to your products (Figure 1.4).

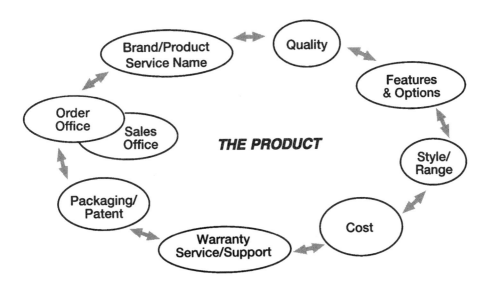

Figure 1.4   The product

- **The elements of PRICE** Price can be one of the most effective weapons in the marketing armoury. Develop a pricing policy and use it wisely as part of your marketing mix (Figure 1.5).

Figure 1.5   The price

- **The PROMOTION method** The elements of promotion mix represents how you communicate with your target groups. Evaluate all communication avenues not just media advertising (Figure 1.6).

Figure 1.6   The promotion

- **Your PLACE in the market** Place is used to represent the position of your product or service in its market place and also the importance of it being physically available when required (Figure 1.7).

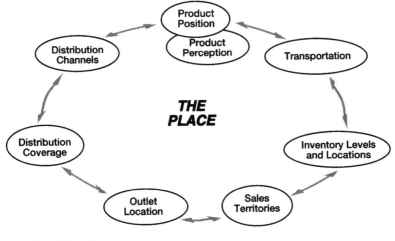

Figure 1.7   The place

- **The PEOPLE mix** Everybody can become an ambassador for your company or product. How good are the employees, associates or agents who deal with your customers (Figure 1.8)?

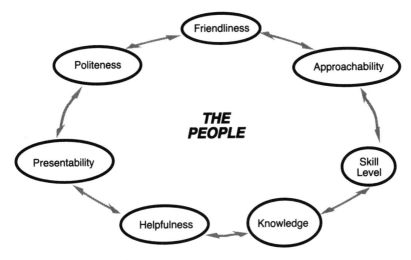

Figure 1.8   The people

- **The PROCESS mix**   The process 'P' is self explanatory. Does it matter if you keep people waiting? Are your application forms or service response times as good as you would like (Figure 1.9)?

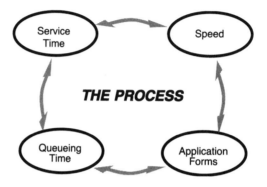

Figure 1.9   The process

- **The PRESENCE**   The presence relates to the buildings or the environment that your customers associate with you (Figure 1.10).

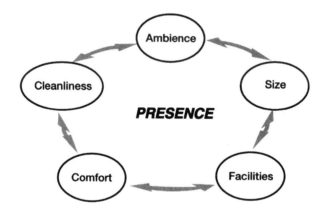

Figure 1.10   The presence

■ The Marketing Planning Process

There are seven major steps in the marketing planning process, each of which is discussed in more detail in later chapters of this book:

1. Establish your present position – where are you now?

2. Complete an internal audit – what have you got?

3. Undertake an external audit – how big is your market? Who are your competitors?

4. Determine the marketing mix – what do you need to do?

5. State the objective – what do you want to achieve?

6. Prepare the marketing plan – how do you get where you want to go?

7. Monitor review and revise – are you still going in the right direction?

Figure 1.11 illustrates these steps.

Figure 1.11 The marketing planning process

■ The Marketing Tools

The fourth component of marketing is a range of techniques and activities. The marketing techniques that can be used to help a business plan and implement its strategy successfully include:

- Market research.
- Competitor analysis.
- Market size and market share measurement.
- Economic modelling and forecasting.
- Sales forecasting and forward planning.
- Product and brand management.
- New product development procedures.
- Marketing communications planning.
- Media planning.
- Monitoring and analysing performance.
- Measuring variations from the norm.

1. **Market Research** Everybody knows something about market research – even if it is just about opinion polls. All businesses should use some form of research in their work. If you are a very local business you will use your local knowledge to find things out, but if you want to sell to a wider market, either regionally, nationally or internationally, then you will need access to research information. The main forms of research are:

- *Desk research* Probably the most important form of research is desk research. Libraries are nearly always a good source of information on your market. You should always try to find out whether a suitable market report exists before initiating your own programme of research.

- *Quantitative research* Quantitative research is the way to find out about your market. How many customers, how often do they buy and how big is the market?. It usually consists of presenting a questionnaire to a sample of users and potential users of a product. The results are generally analysed using computer programs.

- *Qualitative research* Qualitative research is used to develop ideas – users' detailed opinions are sought through interviews or discussion groups.

Chapter 4 provides further information on research techniques and sources.

2. **Competitor Analysis** Do you know who your competitors are?

- How big are they?
- What do they charge?

● How do they market?

You cannot really compete without knowing your competitors.

As well as analysing your competitors you should take the opportunity to analyse your own enterprise and its competitiveness. You will need to ask yourself the vitally important question – why should anybody buy from us rather than from someone else? If you cannot think of a single reason you really do have a problem! Purchasers are asking themselves this question and if there is no good reason to use you then they won't!

When you have assessed your own qualities and those of your competitors you will have a better understanding of how to market your enterprise effectively.

3. **Market Size and Market Measurement**   It is important to know how big your market is and whether it is growing or contracting. If there is no published information on your market it is fairly easy to use your experience to make a rough estimate.

Although we will discuss this later it is important to consider relevant market size. For example, if you are a newsagent in Blackpool it hardly matters to you that the total UK CTN (confectionary, tobacco and newspaper) market is £6500 million only that the total market you can reach is, say, £2 million (you can work it out approximately by ratioing the number of UK households against the number of households you can reach from your shop). What is your share or potential share?

You might be a printer with two markets – jobbing print, (that is, letterheads and so on and colour print: four-colour brochures and so on). The market for jobbing print would be truly local, with a 10- or 15-mile-radius catchment area and a total market of £2 million or £3 million, whilst the four-colour print market that you could service could stretch over the whole of a region or county and be a market worth hundreds of millions of pounds.

4. **Economic Modelling and Forecasting**   No man is an island and our businesses are very much affected by factors beyond our control. This is often called the macro environment.

Many companies have developed models that forecast sales based on outside factors, such as price, income and competitor activity and so on. Simple models may help you predict sales and hence stock ordering – a local newsagent notes the weather and is able to relate video hiring to weather in the summer. This approach can be useful for forecasting takings and so on.

5. **Sales Forecasting and Forward Planning**   Economic modelling is part of this process and the two should be considered together. Forecasting is important in that the process indicates what resources such as stock and staff you will require, whether you will have cash flow problems and so on.

6. **Product and Brand Management**   Small companies will not be able to afford a separate person for product or brand management, but someone needs to be responsible for all the elements of the product or brand, including:

*   Quality of product

*   Sourcing of raw material

*   Packaging

*   Pricing

7. **New Product Development**   Companies should always be seeking to add new products to their portfolio to replace products that go out of fashion or become technologically obsolete.

How many of us have reel-to-reel tape recorders as the main part of our audio system? The answer is very few, yet twenty years ago all serious hi-fi enthusiasts had a reel-to-reel recorder. Many of these were made by Akai, and if Akai had not introduced new products it would not have grown as a company because the use of reel-to-reel declined with the growth of cassette machines.

Akai now make high-quality video recorders (and continue to provide reel-to-reel sound recorders for professional users), thereby capitalising on its reputation for high-quality products and utilising its technical reel-to-reel skills.

8. **Market Communications and Media Planning**   How can anyone buy your product if they don't know about it? Marketing communication includes:

*   *Communications channels* such as advertising, public relations, sponsorship, exhibitions.

*   *Media planning*, which includes allocating resources, determining the timing and choosing appropriate media, such as TV, radio, posters, press, journals, display, classified.

*   *Communication message*: telling people what you want them to know.

All these elements are important and will be explained in more detail later in this book.

9. Monitoring and analysing performance and measuring variations from the norm Once a plan is developed, progress should be measured on a regular basis. This gives early warning of problems and enables action to be taken to get the company back on plan.

CHAPTER 2

Market Appraisal: The Internal Audit

It is almost impossible to run a business without a business plan. If there are no objectives and goals, how can you know you are making the right decision?

By logical extension the same is true of marketing. Indeed you have to have a good, well-developed marketing plan with a clearly defined objective before you make a business plan, as good marketing is at the heart of all good businesses. It is not possible to create a plan without knowledge of your business and its market.

The planning process is a disciplined one and comprises a number of stages, including an internal audit of your business, which helps you to determine your present position, and an external audit, which covers all aspects of the market in which your business operates, such as size, competition and trends.

Some parts of the internal audit are often omitted by larger companies as not being a part of marketing, but they certainly need to be part of the business and market planning routine for smaller businesses. Subjects to address include (optional items are asterisked):

- Company structure*
- Overheads*
- Customer base
- Production and distribution costs
- Sales and marketing methods and costs

■ Company Structure

If there is just one of you then the business has a very simple structure! Once there are two of you it is important to decide who does what so that vital functions are not ignored and you don't find that both of you are attending to the same matters, or neither of you are attending to them, thereby wasting time and money.

If your business is reasonably big with say twenty or so employees, when you try to draw an organisational chart you may find that everybody reports directly to you. You need to try to reduce this direct reporting and share the load amongst your more senior colleagues.

An illustration of this type of flat management structure is shown in Figure 2.1, as is the more conventional devolved organisational structure.

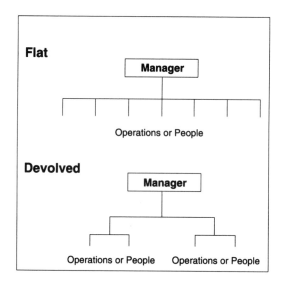

Figure 2.1   Organisational structures

■ Overheads

People spend far too much time forecasting overheads – at the end of the day they will not be very different from those of last year. You should not include sales and marketing costs in overheads – these are discretionary and should be shown before overheads (more on this in Chapter 14).

■ Customer Base

As you will learn in Chapter 13 on customer care, retaining and nurturing your customers is more efficient than trying to recruit new ones. In order to keep your customer base it is important to know as much as you can about them:

- How many customers do you have?

- What is their order frequency? (Daily, weekly or monthly?)

- Are some (as usually happens) more important to you than others? If so, what percentage?

- What type of businesses are they in?

- Where are they located?

- What do you know about your main customers?

Try to complete the following table.

Key customers	Type of business	Location	Order of frequency	% of your business

If you have the answers to these questions you are on the way to successful customer care. If you do not know the answers you need to do something to redress this weakness.

After completing the analysis of your customer base you should take some time out to consider the *potential customer base*. This will consist of two types:

- **More of the same**: look at the customer type with whom you are most successful and see how you can find more of the same (Chapter 8 on targeting will help).

- **Different types**: are there enterprises with which you do not trade that could use your services or products? You might end up uncovering a whole new market for your business.

■ Production and Distribution Costs

Close analysis will lead you to consider whether you can reduce your cost base by more efficient manufacture (better systems, mechanisation, contract manufacture) and distribution (better delivery routes, different carrier and so on).

■ Sales and Marketing Methods and Costs

This is where the internal and external audit meet (Figure 2.2).

- Have you analysed what sales you are getting for each pound spent on selling?

- Are all sales persons or methods as efficient as each other?

- Are you concentrating on the most fruitful customer type?

- Is your advertising appropriate to your regional spread and customer base?

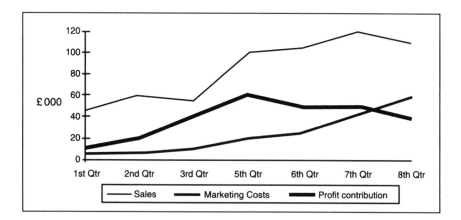

Figure 2.2   Sales and marketing costs, and contributions to other overheads

The questions you need to answer include the following.

What were total sales in the last financial period?

Sales £ [   ] Average sales per product range £ [   ]

Marketing £ [   ] Average marketing costs per £ [   ]
costs sales person or retail outlet

Total sales £ [   ] Average selling costs per sales £ [   ]
force costs person or retail outlet

Average sales per person/outlet £ [   ]

Sales volume from the best £ [   ]

Sales volume from the worst £ [   ]

What percentage of total sales do your top 20 per cent of % [   ]
customers produce?

How is your advertising budget spent?

Media	£	Campaign title
. . . .	. . . .	. . . .
. . . .	. . . .	. . . .
. . . .	. . . .	. . . .
. . . .	. . . .	. . . .

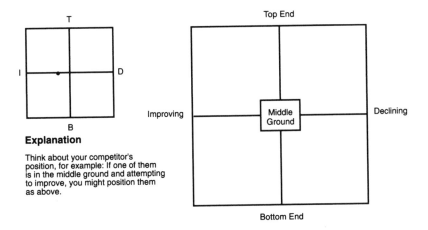

Explanation

Think about your competitor's position, for example: If one of them is in the middle ground and attempting to improve, you might position them as above.

Figure 3.6   (1) Competitors' perceived positions

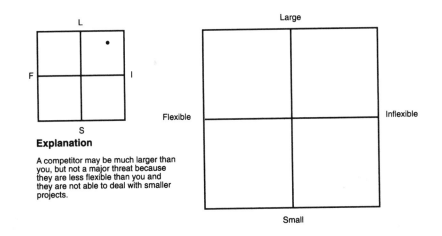

Explanation

A competitor may be much larger than you, but not a major threat because they are less flexible than you and they are not able to deal with smaller projects.

Figure 3.6   (2) Competitor size

CHAPTER 3

Market Appraisal: The External Audit

The external audit analyses those topics considered to be conventional marketing issues, such as:

- Market definition.

- Market size.

- Market segmentation.

- User profile.

- Company and product or service images.

- Competitors: size, products and services.

- Relative positioning.

- Pricing and discounts of your products and those of competitors.

Some of the above need to be commented on as they may be new to you and there are some issues to be discussed.

■ Market Definition

Defining your market is important because it affects how you react to change. At some times market definitions are clear but at others they are not. Consider the following:

- If you are one of the town's retail bakers your market is the retail bread market in your town. If you sell fish and chips – your market is not just fish and chips (as it once was), but all take-away food; your competitors are not just other fish and chip shops but all of the many outlets in your area that sell take-away food, such as pizzas, Indian and Chinese.

- If in the 1950s you sold ocean liner passages across the Atlantic would you have thought you needed to start selling airline tickets as well? Did your customers want to sail the Atlantic or just to travel from London to New York? The answer may have been either or both.

- The same applied to retailers of radios and gramophones – now they sell televisions, videos and CD players. In hindsight this progression may be obvious but sometimes the future is not always so easy to predict.

Ask yourself what are you providing and what is the market?

A business man we know said he has no competitors in the area for his
Go Kart track because there are no other Go Kart racing tracks in the area,
but in fact he is competing against all the other leisure attractions in the area
which appeal to his clients. *His market is leisure activities.*

It is important to be able to define your market, your competititors and everybody's relative position in the market place. The first step is to consider carefully the market or markets in which you are operating and complete the following table. The markets we operate in are:

1	
2	
3	
4	

■ Market Size

Now that you have defined your market it is important to work out its size.

Sources of marketing information (see later) will tell you what percentage of the population, often by age and sex, use your service or buy your product. It is not too difficult to find out about your local population demographics and work out how many are potential clients.

Obtaining market information can be very important, as the following example illustrates.

Another business person we know, a prospective retailer of gifts for young people, when planning to open a new retail outlet suddenly realised that the business would have very limited potential because it was based in a town with a small youth population. *This retailer had to rethink strategy and consider whether to proceed at all!*

Your market size will depend upon the geographic area the business could cover – you should know that from your customer analysis. If you can extend your business catchment area the potential market size increases. Also, if you know what the average customer spends per year, then you can estimate the market size. You need to do this for each market you operate in, using a checklist similar to the one below. Anyone selling into large markets needs this discipline to help focus marketing activity.

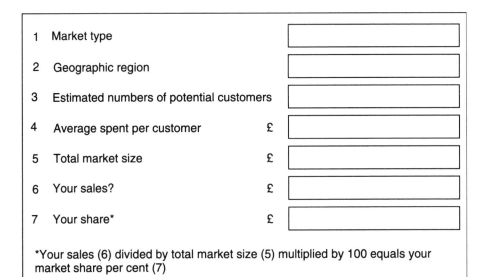

1	Market type		
2	Geographic region		
3	Estimated numbers of potential customers		
4	Average spent per customer	£	
5	Total market size	£	
6	Your sales?	£	
7	Your share*	£	

*Your sales (6) divided by total market size (5) multiplied by 100 equals your market share per cent (7)

Market share (%)	Growing market	Falling market
1 to 5	Work on it	Get out
6 to 15	Healthy	Problems
16+	Doing well	Watch out

Figure 3.1   How big is your market?

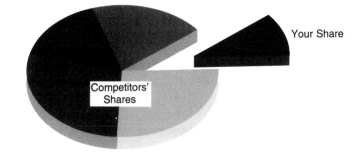

Figure 3.2   Are you keeping your share?

If you have got a small share and the market is growing, then go for it! At the other end of the scale, if you have got a large share either you will have trouble expanding your business or you will find that your competitors are after some of your business and are nibbling away at your share.

It has been suggested that if you have a business of a size that is comfortable for you then you should not necessarily be looking to increase your share. If this is what you want then take care not to get swept aside by an aggressive competitor. *You might have to fight just as hard to hold your ground.*

■ Market Segmentation

This is a technique that divides a market into significant parts and allows you to concentrate on the parts relevant to you. Segmentation can be by product type or user, depending upon what is considered useful.

The car market is one that is segmented by car type, and each of the segments is a battle ground for the various cars and makers. For example, consider the two opposite ends of the car market:

- Luxury cars: Jaguar, Mercedes, BMW, Lexus, Rolls Royce and so on.

- Compacts: AX, Clio, Corsa, Mini, Fiesta, Micra, 106 and so on.

The types of buyer in the luxury car market and the ways to reach them should be entirely different from the way in which the compact car manufacturers market their wares.

Examples of market segmentation can also be found in the professional sector. An accountancy firm would have different types of business, as follows:

Type of business	Type of client
Full audit accounts	Limited companies above a certain size
Incomplete accounts	Small businesses and partnerships
Tax returns	Private clients or partners

If you consider these segmentation groups then you will realise that to increase business each segment will require a different marketing approach.

■ How Does Your Market Segment?

How would you define the segments of your market and the users of each segment (they may be one and the same)? Complete the market segmentation table below.

Market segment	Users
. . . .	. . . .
. . . .	. . . .
. . . .	. . . .
. . . .	. . . .
. . . .	. . . .
. . . .	. . . .
. . . .	. . . .
. . . .	. . . .

You will need to do this exercise for each of the market segments in which you operate. You will also need to do it for any segments that are potential new markets for you.

■   Image, Position and Perception

Image and position are an integral part of market definition. The customer's perception of a brand or company is the result of the company's investment in product and service quality and how it has projected this image through advertising and other forms of communication.

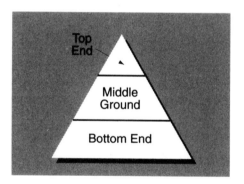

Figure 3.3   Three-section marketing triangle

There are different market sectors to exploit profitability (Figure 3.3). Put simply, there is:

- The top end: a small and exclusive group that requires the best and does not care what it pays.
- The middle ground: those seeking quality and value for money.
- The bottom end: those requiring a basic product at the lowest price.

Having chosen your position in the market place, it is important to project the right image for what you are trying to achieve. Consistency is vital and inappropriate activity should be avoided. For example no one would consider selling Rolls Royce cars using a cash-back promotion, would they?

If there is a difference between your chosen position and your customers' perception of your business, you may overvalue your worth in the market place or even undervalue and probably underprice yourself. Research will help tell you if this is the case.

If you are serving tea you can do it from Spode China, Denbyware or a polystyrene cup. You still get to drink the tea! It doesn't affect the tea but it gives a different impression, the better the presentation, the better the impression made on the drinker and *the better the price you can get for the cuppa!*.

Returning to the car market, the following selection of motor manufacturers shows how they have attempted to position themselves (Figure 3.4).

As expected, in the UK the middle ground is very crowded and you might question some of the positionings. If you do, this is because your perception of their positions is different from those of the manufacturers. Remember what we said?

> Where the manufactures think they are will be reflected in their marketing and especially their advertising.

Two interesting examples of repositioning in recent years are the different approaches adopted by Honda and Toyota, both of whom are known throughout the world as mass producers of cheap and reliable small cars.

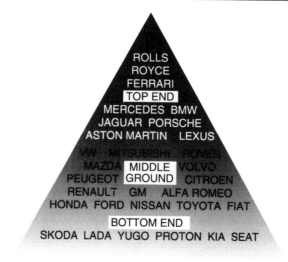

Figure 3.4   Graded triangle

To move up-market Honda developed a strategy based on engineering excellence, promoted heavily through the Grand Prix motor racing circuit. This successful strategy has helped them move from the 'bottom end' of the segmentation scale to the higher-value 'top end' with a range of cars and prices that now compete directly with the likes of Mercedes and BMW.

Toyota adopted an entirely different strategy and from a standing start decided simply to build one of the best 'top end' cars ever made. To overcome resistance of the perceived Toyota image among the upper segments of the market a new marque, 'Lexus', was introduced and marketed differently from Toyota's other models. In just a few years the Lexus has been accepted as one of the world's luxury cars and is claimed to be the most reliable car in its class.

Daewoo, another new car manufacturer is now trying to develop its image in the UK market. Where would you position them on the segmentation triangle?

Now that you have considered your market place, its size, competitors and the various segments within it, mark the position you think you have achieved (Figure 3.5).

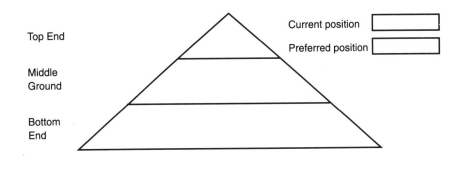

Top End

Middle
Ground

Bottom
End

Current position

Preferred position

Figure 3.5   Marketing triangle

Is this the position you want? If not mark the position you would like to achieve.

■ **What Image Do You Project to Your Customers?**

Which of the following image components applies to you?

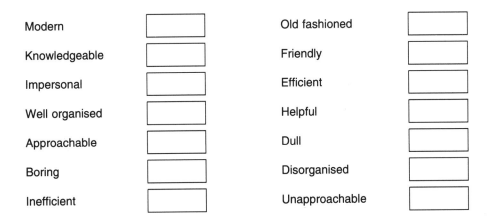

Modern		Old fashioned	
Knowledgeable		Friendly	
Impersonal		Efficient	
Well organised		Helpful	
Approachable		Dull	
Boring		Disorganised	
Inefficient		Unapproachable	

Perhaps you don't know, but you should!

What about your competitors? Can you complete the following?

Competitor	Size (L, M or S*)	Position (T M B**)	Image components

* Large, medium or small.
** Top, middle or bottom.

If you are not able to complete the above it is because you do not have the necessary information. Any military strategist or successful businessman will emphasise how important it is to know your enemy (or in this case competitor) if you want to be sure of success.

■ Competitor Evaluation

Now you should be able to evaluate your competitors using the three matrices below (Figures 3.6(1), (2) and (3)).

CHAPTER 4

Market Appraisal: Research

If you have questions that need answering or you want to find things out you need to do some research. There are two main forms of research: desk research and field research:

- **Desk research** is sourcing information and answers from printed publications, electronic media and your own internal resources. This is always the first place to start any research process and you may be surprised at the amount of relevant information revealed.

- **Field research** is invariably more expensive than desk research and careful planning is needed at all stages to ensure that the research project is actually proceeding without bias, within budget and is likely to produce informative answers. The two main types of field research are *quantitative research* and *qualitative research*. As their names suggest, quantitative research counts things (how many? how often? and so on). Qualitative research elicits opinions, ideas to help identify trends or develop new products.

The questions you need to answer are invariably who, why, when, where, what and how:

- Competition:
    - *What* do you know about your competition?
    - Do you know *who* they are?
    - Do you know *what* they do?
    - Do you know *what* they charge?
    - Do you know *how* they market, sell and promote?
- Customers:
    - *What* do you know about your customers?
    - *Who* are they?
    - *Why* do they buy your products?
    - *When* do they buy your products?
    - *Where* are they?

- – *What* do they do?
- – *What* do they think of you?
- – *What* do they think of your competitors?

- Market:

  - – *How* big is your market?
  - – *How* is it growing?
  - – *How* does it vary regionally?

How can you find the answers to these questions?

- Competitors: Ring them up, get their brochures, look for their adverts.

- Customers: Analyse records, send them a questionnaire.

- Market: Go to the library – read a report by Mintel, EIU, Keynote, Retail Business (see end of chapter for sources). Most big city public libraries have a commercial section. Additionally TECs, trade and industry centres, Business Links, trade associations and chambers of commerce carry or have access to relevant information.

■ Quantitative Research

Before you market your product you may want to know what proportion of the public in all parts of the country are likely to purchase your product or service. Conducting a national survey is expensive but all large research companies such as Gallup, Marplan and BMRB run an omnibus service and you can arrange for just a few questions to be asked all over the country at a very reasonable cost.

If you decide you need a more local survey you can do it yourself, but be careful not to bias the sample in such a way as to make the results over-favourable.

■ Qualitative Research

This is a development from a psychological treatment whereby mentally ill people – mainly schizophrenics – were encouraged to talk about their problems (remember 'One Flew over the Cuckoo's Nest?'). The techniques probably helped many patients but indirectly it gave birth to a very successful industry – qualitative research.

In a research group members of the public are recruited to talk about any aspect of a product or service and its marketing. Recent developments have been in the application of qualitative research to customer service in retail stores. This is a technique you could easily adapt by holding a customer evening and inviting them along to comment on your products and services.

■ Researching Your Market

In order to target your customers as accurately as possible you need to know as much as possible about the market in which you operate. In many cases some form of original research will be required, but before you commit yourself to what could be a time-consuming project you should always determine what published research is available for you to use.

Consumer markets will nearly all be covered by the TGI (Target Group Index), which will tell you how many consumers are active in your market plus demographics and many behavioural measures. In addition Mintel or Retail Business may have produced a study of your market. Other sources of consumer information are major media providers such as regional TV companies or publishing groups.

Industry data for commercial studies should begin with production statistics from the Government Statistical Service and industry surveys. All production statistics from a sample of manufacturers in the UK are collected and collated with Customs and Excise import and export data by the CSO (Central Statistical Office), based at Newport, Gwent. This information is published quarterly by SIC (Standard Industrial Classification) code and can provide quite detailed information on the size and structure of a market.

Because these publications, called PQs (business monitors), have been produced for many years they are very useful as an aid to economic forecasting and for identifying long-term trends such as declining industries, rising imports, and increasing or decreasing UK consumer consumption.

ICC Business Publications is an organisation that produces detailed financial ratios and other information on industries by analysing company reports. For trade and industrial studies, trade associations and their trade publications are an invaluable source of data and information on other data sources, such as commercial databases.

■ Commercial Databases as Sources of Information

Numerous commercial data bases exist as sources of information. The amount of information available is staggering. For example two million names are available from Mardev and a similar number from Listshop.

The Mardev list has 20 'psychodemographic' sort variables as well as regional selection and Acorn 'discriminators', which in turn have up to twenty sort variables, so it should be possible to target those you want fairly accurately (if perhaps rather expensively).

EMAP Direct offers lists of the readers of their ten computer and financial magazines, such as *PC User*, *Minicomputer News* and *Money Week*. This list can be broken down by geographical and other selectors.

British Investors Database lists the 5 per cent of the population that controls 60 per cent of the wealth and covers 2.5 million households. Some fifty breaks are possible on this list.

The Financial Times Business List offers addresses of purchasers of high-cost management and industry reports, purchasers of *Investors Chronicle* and so on.

Dunn & Bradstreet's *Dunn's Marketing* has 400 000 actively trading world-wide businesses on file. Selections are available by SIC code, size of business (employees, turnover, age of business), one named executive and so on.

Market Location has 50 000 businesses in the UK by SIC code.

Other well known commercial sources are *Kompass* and *Yellow Pages*, which are also available in computerised form.

This is just a small example of the available databases. Any list broker such as Mail Marketing, Profords or KPM will be able to tell you what lists are available and would be suitable for your business. In addition most trade publications provide a mailing list in exchange for a fee. The quality varies depending on the source, but some form of sorting criterion is often included.

■ Online Databases and the Internet

Conventional databases can be obtained in the form of computer printouts, mailing labels and computer files or are available on CD ROM. In addition a range of databases can be accessed via the Internet. These include Prestel, Harvest, Textline and Mead.

Mead Data Central International has two main products: LEXIS, a legal database, and NEXIS, a business database. These databases are vast, containing over three million published articles.

DIALOG is a huge database host, offering access to 400 public databases such as statistical files, press wire services and corporate finance.

Other online data bases such as Reuters can also give immediate access to financial market prices.

Many businesses now operate on a worldwide basis using the Internet. This whole world of information exchange is becoming well-developed and is proving increasingly useful to businesses, both to obtain information and for the worldwide marketing of specialist products and services.

The Internet is the world's fastest developing communication system and anyone with a modern pc, a modem and telephone can connect to it. As a result messages can be sent worldwide, often for just the cost of a local telephone call. One of the key features of the Internet is the World Wide Web, which provides an easy to use graphical interface between computers. Information pages can be set up either by buying a site or by using one of the many site providers, and for a small cost your information can be read by anyone in the world. Lists of service providers are becoming available in local directories and new Internet publications are appearing every day.

■ Sources of Mailing Lists

Hamilton House Mailings Limited, 17 Stavely Way, Brixworth Industrial Park, Northampton, NN6 9EL. Tel: (01604) 881889, Fax: (01604) 880735. Education, professional, named persons by industry or commerce, industry by type, commerce by type, health, local government, education by type. Also for consumer lists by lifestyle indicators.

Profords Associates, Profords House, 56 Earl Howe Road, Holmer Green, Bucks, HP15 6QT. Tel: (01494) 714272, Fax: (01494) 714889. Commercial, industrial, retail and some European mailing lists.

Portland Software, Portland House, Beaumont Close, Biddulph, Staffs, ST8 6TE. Tel/Fax: (01782) 514289. Clubs, churches, associations, leisure and entertainment.

Computer Software & PC Software Guides, Dryden Hennell Publishing, Middle Barn, Bredlands Lane, Canterbury, CT2 0HD. Tel/Fax: (01491) 574671. Lists all current PC and system software.

Personnel Directors/Managers List, Temple Leary Advertising, 34 Buckingham Gardens, West Molesey, Surrey, KT8 1TH. Tel: (0181) 979091, Fax: (0181) 9412730. List of directors and senior managers.

Management & Business Consultants in the UK, Searchline Publishing, Searchline House, Bull Lane, Chislehurst, Kent, BR7 6NY. Tel: (0181) 467180, Fax: (0181) 2951759. List of consultants, market retail and consumer.

■ Market Retail and Consumer Surveys

The Key Note Manager, Key Note Publications Ltd, Field House, 72 Oldfield Road, Hampton, Middlesex, TW12 1BR. Tel: (0181) 7830755. Consumer surveys and customer profiles.

The British Shopper 1992/93, NTC Publications Ltd, Farm Road, Henley-on-Thames, Oxfordshire, RG9 1EJ. Tel: (01491) 574671, Fax: (01491) 571188. Retail and consumer surveys, demographic data.

The Retail Pocket Book, NTC Publications Limited, Farm Road, Henley-on-Thames, Oxfordshire, RG9 1EJ. Tel: (01491) 574671, Fax: (01491) 571188. Lists all retail groups, cash and carries, UK demographics, trade statistics.

Retail Directory of the UK, Newman Books Ltd, Freepost, 32 Vauxhall Bridge Road, London, SW1V 2SS. Tel: (0171) 9736402, Fax: (0171) 2335056. Lists retailers.

Health Care Information Services, 12 Riverview Grove, London, W4 3QJ. Tel: (0181) 9948791, Fax: (0181) 7422418. Data on health care market: NHS trusts, private, local authority; trends in health care delivery.

BMRB, 79–81 Uxbridge Road, Ealing, London, W5 55U. Tel: (0181) 566 5000. TGI and omnibus research.

Marplan, 6/7 Grosvenor Place, London, SW1X 7SH. Tel: (0171) 235 2014. Omnibus research.

NOP, Tower House, Southampton Street, London, WC2E 7HN. Tel: (0171) 612 0100. Omnibus research, especially political.

■ **Industrial and Business to Business. Market Surveys and Company Profiles**

ICC Business Publications, Field House, 72 Oldfield Road, Hampton, Middlesex, TW12 2HQ. Tel: (0181) 7830922, Fax: (0181) 7831940. Company reports, industry sector comparisons.

BRAD Advertiser & Agency List, Maclean Hunter Ltd, Maclean Hunter House, Chalk Lane, Cockfosters Road, Barnet, Herts, EN4 0BU. Tel: (0181) 9759759, Fax: (0181) 4409930. Lists all UK media, newspapers, TV, radio, business publications and consumer publications.

The Marketing Pocket Book, NTC Publications Ltd, Farm Road, Henley-on-Thames, Oxfordshire, RG9 1EJ. Tel: (01491) 574671, Fax: (01491) 571188. Key marketing data.

Jordan & Sons Limited, 21 St. Thomas Street, Bristol, BS1 6JS. Tel/Fax: (0117) 9230600. Industry surveys and company reports.

Kompass, Reed Information Services Limited, Windsor Court, East Grinstead House, East Grinstead, West Sussex, RH19 1XD. Tel: (01342) 326972, Fax: (01342) 317241. Regional reports, industrial companies.

Dunn & Bradstreet Ltd, Holmers Farm Way, High Wycombe, Bucks, HP12 4UL. Tel: (01494) 422000, Fax: (01494) 422260. 400 000 businesses.

Market Location Limited, 1 Warwick Street, Leamington Spa, Warwickshire, CV32 5LW. Tel: (01926) 450388,
Fax: (01926) 430590. Industry lists.

Who else can you think of who could provide you with useful information?

```
.................................................................................................
.................................................................................................
.................................................................................................
```

CHAPTER 5

Market Appraisal: The Marketing Mix Matrix

Each marketing mix is unique to a particular business. Because strategic objectives and available resources will differ it is highly unlikely that any two businesses, even direct competitors, would consider the marketing mix in exactly the same way and consequently develop identical marketing plans.

The concept of the seven Ps of the marketing mix was introduced in Chapter 1. Use the marketing mix matrix in this chapter to help determine the importance of each element to your business. There are seven matrix tables to complete, one for each P. Once you have identified the elements of each that you consider to be the most relevant to you list them in order of importance on the summary table at the end of this chapter.

Before you can begin to develop a detailed marketing plan it is essential to have a clear understanding of the value of the above components to your current business and what effect changing the emphasis of the mix would have on future business. Here are a few 'P' points to think about.

■ The Product

■ Quality

Not every product needs to be of the highest quality – yours should be as good as the market expects, or as good as you can make it for the cost. Whatever the quality level, it is important that standards are set and maintained consistently.

Over the years many standards have been introduced in an effort to improve manufacturing performance, product quality and employee skills. These include:

- QC & I (quality control and inspection).
- BSI & DIN (British Standards Institute & German Standards Institute).

- SPC (statistical process control).

- JIT (just in time).

- QC (quality circles).

- TQM (total quality management).

- ISO 9000 (European manufacturing standard).

- BS5750 (UK quality standard).

- BS EN ISO 9000 (extension of ISO 9000 to other businesses).

- NVQ (national vocational qualifications; new training standards).

Historically most of these standards have tended to dictate and control rather than encourage self-development. Industries have had different standards and this has often meant that it has been difficult to compare product quality or gauge the ability of a potential employee trained in one business sector and applying to work in a different one. Now with NVQs and GNVQs national standards are being established for the workplace, for manufacturing, businesses and other types of organisations, and for individuals.

What quality standards do you want to achieve in your business?

```
....................................................................................................
....................................................................................................
....................................................................................................
```

■ **Features and Options**

How important are these? Do your products have special features? Do you need to offer a range of options? Make sure these are known to your customers. Consider which give you an advantage and which ones are missing from your product range.

■ **Style and Range**

Is your range sufficient or even too large? Should you be changing your style?

■ Brand/Product/Service Name

Your name is very important. Is it right? Does it help position your product in its market? Is it protected?

■ Packaging

Look at your packaging. Is it right, or does it need to be modified?

■ Patent

Are your products or services protected by patent, trademark or copyright?

■ Warranty/Service Support

As you will read later, when goods and services are similar the supplier that provides the best service support will usually get the business.

■ Cost

It is important to determine the cost of providing your product as accurately as possible. You should include in product costs all elements that relate directly to the product, at the very least materials and labour. You may also include depreciation of machinery and development costs. However care should be taken not to include general overheads as these will sometimes include sales, which contribute to income. This is discussed in more detail in Chapter 13.

■ Sales Office/Order Office

Does your sales office seek orders or do you mainly respond to customer enquiries? Are these one and the same? Is your sales office acting as an order office only and not actually trying to generate any sales?

- **Sales office**: this is where the interaction between sales person and customer is predominately proactive; the sales office makes the first contact with the customer. Examples include telephone canvassing and telesales operations, including those whose prime function is to make new contacts and set up appointments for representatives.

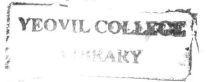

- **Order Office**: this is where the interaction between salesperson and customer is predominantly reactive. That is, the order office sales person more often than not responds to a customer enquiry received by post, fax or phone. Examples include most mail order and catalogue businesses, teletext advertisers and so on.

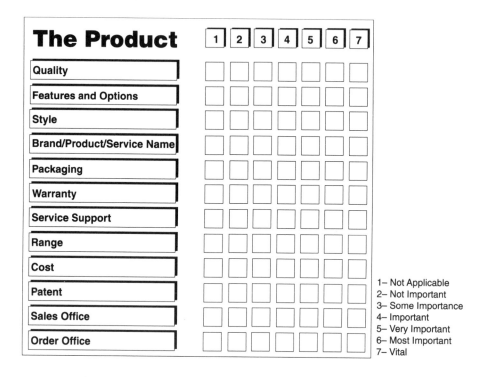

Figure 5.1   Product chart

■ The Price

■ Pricing Level

Many businesses operate a cost-plus policy when it comes to pricing. This can often be an unsatisfactory approach as it may lead to a price level that consumers will not pay or prices that are set well below the market average. If you are more efficient than others in production you should use your advantage wisely, either to make good profits or to compete aggressively. But do not just add a margin to your costs.

■ Pricing Policy

Setting price levels and developing a pricing policy is explained in more detail in Chapter 9.

■ Discounting and Reductions

During the 1980s and early 1990s discounting and, in particular, price reduction were not commonly used as methods of volume gain. Events such as the quality-newspaper price war in the UK and the Marlboro cigarette price reduction in the USA help focus attention on this method of business development. Using discounting to gain volume has its dangers in that the turnover lost is all profit.

To operate this type of policy successfully you need a very efficient system, helpful suppliers and adequate funds.

> Using settlement discounts to encourage early or on-time payment again means giving up hard-earned profits and this type of discounting should not be used as a substitute for an effective credit control system.

■ Price Wars

When times are hard and too many products are chasing too few customers it is tempting for any business to cut prices in order to maintain sales revenue. In such a situation price cutting is sometimes necessary as customers with a smaller amount of disposable income tend to trade down while others are reluctant to buy luxuries until they feel that their prospects are going to improve, or are actually improving.

Sometimes price cutting can be used as a useful marketing tool to help clear surplus stock or revive flagging consumer interest in a product. But when it means cutting into your profit margin just to maintain sales volume, price cutting can lead to a dangerous downward spiral as competitors respond with price cuts to match yours. Once started the spiral continues until supply matches demand as companies stop producing, or close, or until the market expands again.

Companies with high fixed costs seek ways of cutting costs in order to maintain profits. The quickest and easiest short-term cuts can be made by cutting product development, marketing, advertising and other indirect costs. However these are often areas where a company needs to maintain expenditure in order to ensure its continuation.

The dangers of price cutting can be demonstrated by the following example.

A business sells 4000 units a month at a list price of £10 with a gross margin of 25 per cent. A competitor's pricing tactics are starting to affect sales and in order to try to maintain unit sales our business starts to cut its prices by 5 per cent.

Unit volume holds up at 4000 units but monthly revenue is reduced by 5 per cent to £38 000.

The £2000 discount has to come from profits, which are now reduced to £8000 and the gross profit margin which was 25 per cent is now reduced to 21 per cent, a fall in the gross profit available to help cover overheads and other costs of 8 per cent.

Two months later the competitor cuts its price again and increases sales. In response our business cuts its price by another 5 per cent but unit volume drops by 5 per cent to 3800 units per month. The buying price and all other costs remain the same.

The unit price is now £9.00 (£10 − 10 per cent) monthly turnover is down to £34 200 (−14.5 per cent). But most importantly, the gross profit is now only £5700 per month − a gross margin of just 16.7 per cent!

At this stage, with break-even of £7500 per month, the business owners finally become aware of the dangerous situation they have got into and call a sales meeting. The owners want to return to £10 000 per month gross profit, but the sales manager does not think that the margin can be improved, although unit sales can be increased. To achieve the gross profit target, what will the new sales level have to be and what per cent increase on current turnover does this represent? (Answer at the end of the chapter.)

This example helps to illustrate the need for a planned approach to pricing and the importance of determining your pricing policy so that you can lead rather than be led.

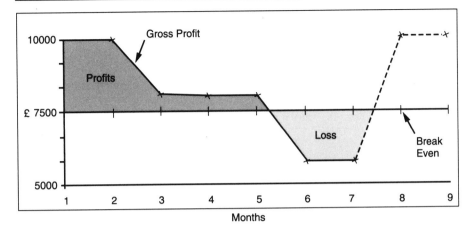

Figure 5.2   Price wars gross profit graph

■ Credit Terms and Payment Methods

Providing terms and payment methods may give you a competitive advantage. Naturally there is a danger in giving too much credit – it eats into your profits and long-term credit can easily turn into bad debt.

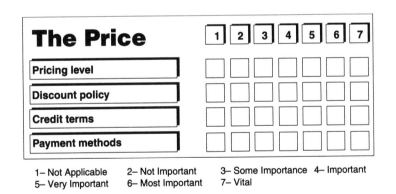

Figure 5.3   Price chart

■ Pricing and Positioning

As we will discuss more fully in Chapter 9, pricing is a very important part of positioning. Our experience is that many small firms underprice their goods and services. They believe they should charge less because they are small and thus undervalue the specialist, personalised service they can offer and larger firms can not.

It is important that your goods or services are consistent with your pricing policy. If your goods are high-quality and luxurious, do not present them in brown paper bags. Alternatively if you are 'green' and economic your customers will not expect gold blocked lettering on your packaging.

Remember the famous pricing curve. Not only does increasing the price lead to reduced sales, so does lowering the price: people cannot accept very low prices – are the goods stolen, are they defective?

A labourer is worthy of his or her time – and your goods and services are worthy of their price!

Figure 5.4   Pricing and positioning bell chart

■ The Place

■ Distribution Channels

What methods do you use to sell your goods – mail order, via supermarkets, factors, direct mail? Are they all as effective as they could be, or should you consider another method?

Most markets have significantly different distribution channels. For groceries these are major multiples, independents, wholesalers and cash and carrys. If you deal with major multiples you will need to make personal representations or use agents. Independents can be contacted directly via your sales team or through wholesalers. Sometimes small independents can be contacted via telesales or mail order.

Most other markets are reached:

- directly for major accounts,

- via factors or wholesalers for smaller accounts.

Knowing the appropriate structure for your industry enables you to market and sell efficiently.

■ Distribution Coverage

How important is your distribution coverage in your operating areas? Are you getting to all the key customers in the market or in each relevant area?

■ Outlet Location

Is your retail outlet in the right place? Should you have one somewhere else – another part of town, another town, another part of the country?

■ Sales Territories

Are your salespersons' territories efficiently chosen?

■ Inventory Levels and Locations

Having the right goods in the right place at the right time can be a vital factor in servicing an account. Having too large a stock of the wrong products can lead to disaster. Conversely being out of stock can cause embarrassment and a possible loss of custom.

■ Transportation

Are you using the right method, the most efficient carrier?

■ **Product Positioning and Perception**

You will have read a whole section on this in Chapter 3 with respect to the external audit.

- *Product positioning* is where you have to place your product in the market place or where you would like to be.

- *Product perception* is where your customers and potential customers perceive you to be in the market place.

Fine if your position and their perception is roughly the same, but if there are differing views, watch out! You could find that sales falter because you have overpriced or overvalued your product, or conversely that your profits are much less than they could have been because your customers' perception of your product is much higher than your own positioning of it and you are underpricing.

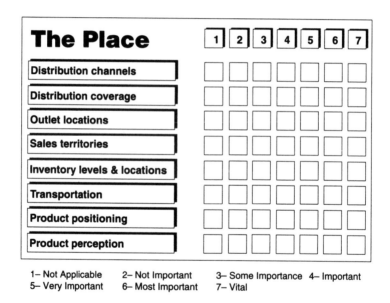

Figure 5.5   Place chart

■ The Promotion

As Chapter 11 on marketing communications will tell you, you will not do any business without promotion. What forms of promotion are best for your business?

- **Advertising**: for most businesses, however small, this activity is vital and is discussed further in Chapter 11 (Marketing Communication).

- **Selling**: a subject worthy of another book, but discussed briefly in Chapter 13 (Customer Care).

- **Promotion**: there are many types of promotion, not just money off – again see Chapter 12.

- **Publicity**: some businesses seem to get their names in the local paper a great deal. Does this help, and how do they do it?

Fill in the following table below before you read Chapters 11 and 12 – you will probably change your scores afterwards!

The Promotion [1] [2] [3] [4] [5] [6] [7]

Advertising							
Selling							
Promotion							
Publicity							

1– Not Applicable 2– Not Important 3– Some Importance 4– Important
5– Very Important 6– Most Important 7– Vital

Figure 5.6   Promotion chart

■ The People

Being nice to people may be overrated as a concept, but a smile is better than a slap in the face.

How important to your business is the quality of your staff? People are no substitute for poor products and services but the wrong people can spoil the impact of all your hard work.

The people 'P' is a list of personal qualities – you just need to consider which are important to your business and how your staff, employees and colleagues rate on these attributes.

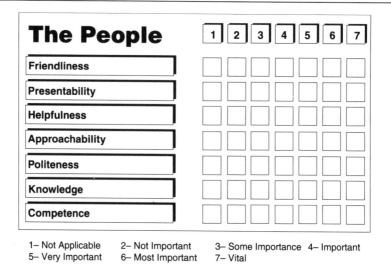

Figure 5.7   People chart

■ The Process

■ Service Time/Speed/Queuing/Waiting Time

Whilst you need to be careful about overstaffing, it is important to deal with enquiries in the shortest possible time. Do substantial queues develop? Customers are intolerant of queuing nowadays.

■ Appointment System

Is it difficult for your customers to gain access to you or make appointments with you? How long does it take for them to get through on the phone? Are you losing business because of blockages here? Do you run to time, or are customers kept waiting?

■ Application Forms

If your business has application forms that clients or customers fill in, are they clear, and do they ask for relevant information?

The Process   [1] [2] [3] [4] [5] [6] [7]

	1	2	3	4	5	6	7
Speed	☐	☐	☐	☐	☐	☐	☐
Efficiency	☐	☐	☐	☐	☐	☐	☐
Service time	☐	☐	☐	☐	☐	☐	☐
Waiting time	☐	☐	☐	☐	☐	☐	☐
Appointment system	☐	☐	☐	☐	☐	☐	☐
Forms and documentation	☐	☐	☐	☐	☐	☐	☐

1– Not Applicable   2– Not Important   3– Some Importance 4– Important
5– Very Important   6– Most Important   7– Vital

Figure 5.8   Process chart

■ The Value of Service as a Marketing Tool

Success in business of any kind depends on satisfying customers. This is a commonsense statement but it is not necessarily common practice even in today's competitive environment.

> In a survey of over 4000 executives, 95 per cent of respondents said that service will become more important in the next five years and 80 per cent believe that service is the key to competitiveness.

When asked to consider in order of importance the factors influencing the buying process, the results were:

1. Quality

2. Reliability & Delivery

3. Problem solving

4. Price

This order of buying influence has been the norm for much of the British manufacturing industry since the mid 1980s. Before that it was:

1. Price

2. Delivery

3. Quality

Another survey in the USA showed that 68 per cent of car and truck buyers who switch to another brand do so because they are disappointed with the service and treatment they receive. Only 14 per cent switched because they preferred the product.

■ Service Excellence

In other words most people are prepared to pay for quality, reliability and experience. Add promptness, a friendly approach and responsive staff who empathise with customers and you can command a higher price than your competitors.

Most of today's industrial and market leaders now recognise that a higher standard of customer service provides them with better returns than their competitors'. In general terms they can achieve:

- Premium prices
- Faster sales growth
- Better profits

So can you!

■ The Presence

Your buildings, shop facades, vehicles and promotional literature indicates to your customers what sort of company you are.

■ Size

What size is your business? How many outlets have you got? How big is your building?

■ Premises

Are these attractive, modern or decrepit?

■ **Corporate Image**

What image does your organisation have? What image do you want it to have? What effort are you making to project this image?

The impression that your organisation gives to potential and actual clients could well affect the amount of business that you do.

■ **Ambience**

What is the atmosphere like in your firm? Is it lively, busy and exciting, or dull and depressing?

■ **Comfort**

Are the places where you receive clients comfortable?

■ **Facilities**

What facilities do you have for different operations?

■ **Cleanliness**

Are your premises clean? No matter what you are doing a high standard of cleanliness always impresses.

The Presence 1 2 3 4 5 6 7

	1	2	3	4	5	6	7
Operational							
Size							
Premises							
Corporate image							
Environment							
Ambience							
Comfort							
Facilities							
Cleanliness							

1– Not Applicable   2– Not Important   3– Some Importance   4– Important
5– Very Important   6– Most Important   7– Vital

Figure 5.9   Presence chart

■ The Components of Your Marketing Mix

Now you have considered the various elements of the marketing mix and how they relate to your product, you need to be able to identify the most important ones and list them in order of importance. Transfer to the form (Figure 5.10) all the sixes and sevens you have ticked previously. These 'P' elements are the vital ones for you. How much attention are you currently paying to them?

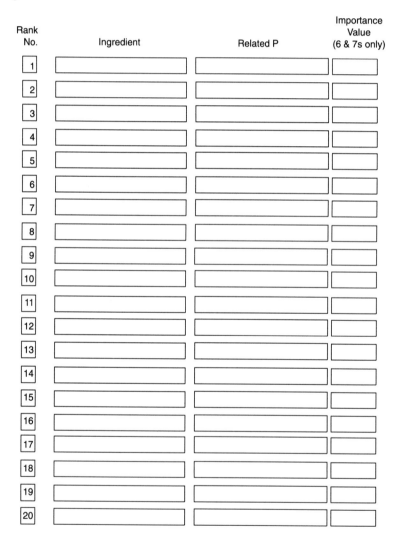

Rank No.	Ingredient	Related P	Importance Value (6 & 7s only)
1			
2			
3			
4			
5			
6			
7			
8			
9			
10			
11			
12			
13			
14			
15			
16			
17			
18			
19			
20			

Figure 5.10   The P ranking chart

■ Answer to problem on page 52.

An increase from £34 200 per month to £59 880 per month, or just over 76 per cent. Can you achieve that level of volume growth in the middle of a price war?

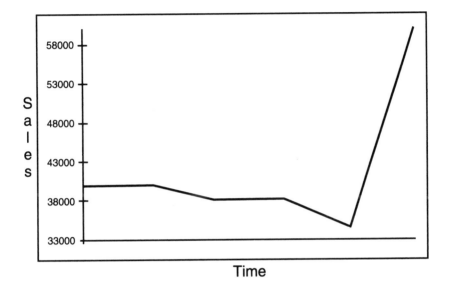

Figure 5.11   Price wars answer chart

If the answer is no – stay out!

CHAPTER 6

Market Appraisal: SWOT Analysis

As well as gathering the information, you have to work out what it means! To help your analysis it is good practice to summarise the situation with a SWOT (Strengths, Weaknesses, Opportunities and Threats) analysis.

The SWOT analysis is very important. It is the process that enables you to assess the present state of your business. What is it? Read on!

- **Strengths**: What the company is good at, the strengths of your product and service, what you do best. Consider how these strengths may be exploited.

- **Weaknesses**: Poor products, services, gaps in the portfolio, image problems. Indicate how these weaknesses may be redressed.

- **Opportunities**: Market growth or change; new markets, products or services; different ways of marketing your products or services.

- **Threats**: Economic forces and competition, changes in legislation, changes of habit. Make contingency plans if possible.

Now try to do a SWOT analysis for your own product, service or company using the SWOT sheets below. Be honest! If you end up with two pages of strengths and no weaknesses you are either very lucky or you are fooling yourself. Remember weaknesses are problems and every problem is an opportunity (that's what the optimists say!).

STRENGTHS:
The strengths of our business are:

These strengths can be
developed further by:

Figure 6.1   SWOT Analysis – Strengths

WEAKNESSES:
The weaknesses of our business or
organisation are:

The steps required to correct
these weaknesses are:

Figure 6.2   SWOT Analysis – Weaknesses

OPPORTUNITIES:
Opportunities that the business or organisation might take advantage of are:

The resources and effort required and the benefit would be:

Resources and effort:

Benefit:

Resources and effort:

Benefit:

Resources and effort:

Benefit:

Figure 6.3   SWOT Analysis – Opportunities

THREATS:
Factors within the business or organisation or from the external environment that could threaten the successful implementation of this plan are:

The steps that can be taken to minimise these threats and the costs involved are:

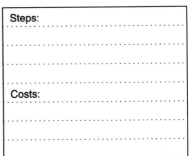

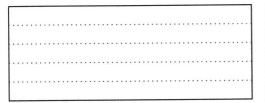

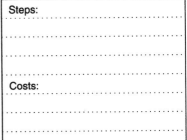

Figure 6.4   SWOT Analysis – Threats

CHAPTER 7

Marketing Planning: Establishing Objectives

■ Objectives

Every business and organisation needs to establish an overall objective, agree the marketing strategy that will help achieve it and prepare the tactical marketing plan that will move the organisation step by step towards the chosen objective. As progress is made the plan is reviewed, the strategy is regularly modified, and when appropriate the objectives are redefined.

What are you aiming to achieve, or What do you want the business to achieve?

- Double your sales?
- Double your profit?
- Stay where you are?
- Just make a profit?

Your objectives may be more detailed than this, defined for each individual product or service, or, if big enough, an individual customer.

Some objectives may not lead directly to increased sales and profit but develop a climate that could help future sales. These objectives, such as heightening product awareness or quality image might be regarded as secondary objectives but this does not make them less important.

Amongst the many reasons for establishing clear aims and objectives within any business environment the following are probably the most important:

- To provide a focus for employees.
- To provide a target that actual achievements can be measured against.
- To provide a basis for planning.
- To provide reassurance to shareholders and potential shareholders.

■ Mission Statement

The 'aims' are often referred to as the mission statement.

> The mission statement is an attempt to define the businesses' philosophy or lifestyle; quite simply, the way a business or organisation proposes to operate.

It can be a simple statement covering perhaps just one main area of operation, such as 'we support green products', or it can encompass the whole gamut of the business operation, including attitudes towards suppliers, customers and employees.

These attitude statements are often called charters but they only relate to one aspect of the organisation, for example the NHS Patients' Charter – they should not be confused with the mission statement, which is meant to encapsulate the entire business.

Do not confuse a mission statement with a vision statement either. The vision statement is how a business would *like* to operate and what it *wishes* to achieve. *The mission statement should reflect reality.*

■ Strategic Business Objectives

Objectives are what a business or organisation wants to achieve within a specific period of time. The strategic business objective or corporate objective is the overall medium- to long-term objective (5, 10 or 15 years).

For businesses, the strategic business objective is usually defined in terms of profitability or a combination of factors such as profitability and market share or market positioning. Non-profit-making organisations often determine their strategic business objective with reference to improved standards, shorter waiting times, increased efficiency or some similarly quantifiable measure.

In order to be achievable the strategic business objective must take account of all the resources required to attain the stated goal, and to do this a series of subordinate objectives need to be defined. These will be determined in conjunction with the various departments, divisions or functions whose performance could affect the overall result. Although there will be differences in emphasis within different organisations, the following will be applicable to most:

- The production objective

- The physical resource objective

- The human resource objective

- The financial resource objective

And of course the subject of this workbook:

- The marketing objective

Once these subordinate objectives have been agreed and defined, then an appropriate strategy for each can be prepared. Each objective is achieved through one or more clearly defined strategies. These subordinate strategies in turn become the objectives for each of the elements of the lower levels of the plan.

■ Marketing Objectives

The marketing objectives are defined so that achieving them enables the overall business objectives to be reached. Clearly if the business objective is to be highly profitable then the objective of achieving a high share with a keen price is unlikely to be compatible with the business objective.

■ The Marketing Strategy

The marketing strategy is how a business or organisation proposes to achieve its marketing objectives.

Constantly changing market conditions mean that marketing strategies have to be reviewed reasonably frequently, and as a result they usually relate to a shorter time period within the framework of the much longer-term strategic business objective. Marketing strategies are usually prepared for 3–5 year periods.

■ The Marketing Plan

Once the marketing strategy has been agreed then the marketing plan can be produced.

The marketing plan is concerned with the tactical moves that are going to be employed. It should detail all that is required to move the business step by step towards the agreed marketing objective. It may also contain a number of strategies, such as sales, promotional and customer care strategies, each with its defined objective. As the diagram at the end of this subsection illustrates, each objective – once determined – requires one or more strategies.

Remember that every time that any objective is reviewed or reconsidered its supporting strategies must be treated likewise.

Once defined it is vital to communicate both your aims and your objectives to help ensure that not only those involved in attaining the objectives are aware of them, but all other relevant people within the organisation are aware also (and sometimes those outside, that is, customers, shareholders or suppliers).

Objectives can and should be set at all levels of business activity and for all operating divisions or departments – but always starting from the highest level and working down to lower levels and communicating with all involved, thus helping to ensure that all the subordinate objectives are compatible with each other and the strategic overview.

Establishing objectives for one part of a business in isolation from its other parts can often be counterproductive, especially if internal communications are poor. A common example of the type of misunderstanding that frequently occurs in all sizes of business is that of the sales manager preparing new sales objectives. He is paid partly on commission and, lacking clear direction from his board, sets a short-term objective that provides for an increase in sales. The sales volume objective is exceeded, albeit at a substantially reduced gross margin than normal. However in reality the overall strategic objective for the period, discussed and agreed by the board but not communicated clearly to other departments, was to increase profits by reducing production costs and maintaining or increasing gross margins even at the expense of sales volume. Result – a good sales manager looking for a job!

The above is just one example of an all too common situation that occurs within businesses and organisation of all sizes, from major multinationals to the small business run by a husband and wife.

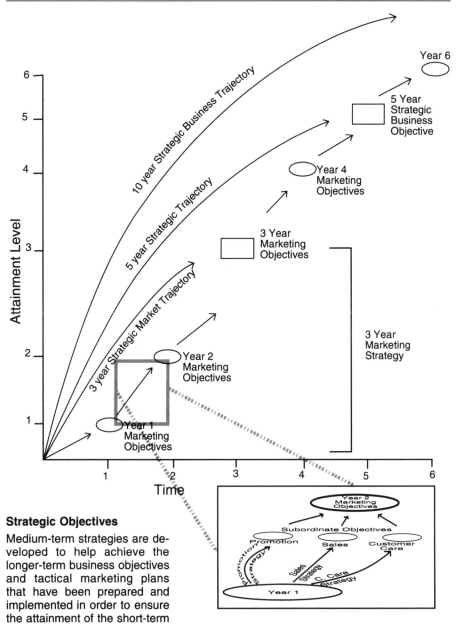

Strategic Objectives

Medium-term strategies are developed to help achieve the longer-term business objectives and tactical marketing plans that have been prepared and implemented in order to ensure the attainment of the short-term marketing objectives. Subordinate objectives are contained within the tactical plan, and these relate to the various plan element: sales, promotions, customer care and so on. Each of these needs its own strategy if the objectives are to be achieved. If any objective is reviewed, all supporting strategies must be treated likewise.

Figure 7.1   Establishing objectives

■ Setting Objectives for Your Business

Remember:

- The mission statement defines *why we are here.*

- The strategic business objective or corporate objective states *where we are going.*

- The strategy – marketing, production, finance or other – defines *how we are going to proceed*, that is the achievable routes available.

- The marketing plan details *the tactical steps that have to be taken* to achieve each stage of the marketing strategy.

At this point you should consider your company and product/service objectives and the strategy that is appropriate for each. (Note that the objectives will become increasingly more specific and their related strategies more detailed.)

If you run a small business do your employees know what objectives you have set and how the business is going to achieve them?

Yes ▢   No ▢

If you are responsible for a marketing or sales function, are you aware of the overall business objective and the marketing objective, and do the objectives you have set take account of these?

Yes ▢   No ▢

Have your objectives been communicated to and agree by all other relevant employees and sections?

Yes ▢   No ▢

If you have ticked 'yes' three times, congratulations, but are you really being honest?

■ The Mission Statement

What is the mission statement for your business?

■ Strategic Objectives

What is the strategic objective of your business or organisation?

Where do you want it to be in five years?

```
..............................................................................
..............................................................................
..............................................................................
```

In ten years?

```
..............................................................................
..............................................................................
..............................................................................
```

Once you have defined your strategic objective you can determine your marketing objectives. Then you can start to construct your marketing plan, detailing the tactics chosen to move you step by step towards your strategic marketing and business objectives. (Note that for many small businesses the strategic marketing and strategic business objectives are often the same.)

A view often expressed is that it is impossible to take a ten-year view when establishing business objectives. We do not agree nor do most people in business, they are happy to take a long-term view and frequently commit themselves to medium- or long-term contracts. We agree that you must continually review your short-term strategy and tactics in order to adjust to current conditions, but you must preserve your overall long-term goal.

■ **Marketing Objectives**

Your marketing objectives are the short- to medium-term steps that help take you closer to your long-term business objective.

What is your marketing objective for the end of your next financial year?

```
..................................................................................
..................................................................................
..................................................................................
```

For three years' time?

```
..................................................................................
..................................................................................
..................................................................................
```

For five years' time?

....
....
....

CHAPTER 8

Targeting

■ The Targeted Approach

Targeting is an important part of planning (Figure 8.1).

Figure 8.1   Bullseye (hit)

Hitting your target with each shot is efficient and cost effective.

■ The Shotgun Approach

To market your product or service to each and every person seems intuitively wrong, and it would be very inefficient (Figure 8.2).

Figure 8.2   Bullseye (miss)

Using the shotgun approach and just aiming in the general direction of your market can be very expensive and often inefficient.

■ The Importance of Targeting

Our aim is to encourage you to use the rifle rather than the shotgun in your attempts to hit the target.

The importance of targeting can be seen by considering some totally inappropriate marketing activities, such as:

- Advertising funeral plans in *Just Seventeen* or *Cosmopolitan*.

- Organising leaflet drops for conservatories and greenhouses at blocks of flats.

We would do neither of these things because they would be inappropriate and a waste of money. So on the positive side it would be sensible to do something that was advantageous! That's why advertisements for funeral plans appear in publications that appeal to older people and leaflet drops for greenhouses and conservatories take place on housing estates.

■ Your Market

You cannot target without knowing what your market is. You may have no trouble defining what it is; alternatively you may have no information at all. You may have a totally new product and will have to decide from whatever evidence you can gather what the most promising targets for your product or service might be, and then how you might reach them. Consider some examples before you read on and see how far you can get:

Product/service	Market	Target market segments
Cheese slices	Cheese	Cheese sandwich makers
One-hour Optician	....	....
Purdey shotguns	....	....
Air tickets	....	....
Battle tanks	....	....

Knowing who the targets are enables more effective marketing to take place.

- **Cheese sandwich makers** will be 'household engineers' who make sandwiches to take to work or for their loved ones to take to work or school. There are some 10 million of these and quite a lot of them read women's magazines and watch commercial television.

- **One-hour opticians** look for people who need spectacles in a hurry. Nearly all people over 50 at least need reading glasses and they watch a lot of television.

- **Purdey shotguns** are very expensive and will be bought by country house owners with unlimited resources. They can be reached through magazines such as *The Field* and *Country Life*.

- **Air ticket sales** is a big market and needs precise definition before targets can be found. If you are marketing first-class business travel then *The Economist*, *Financial Times*, *Management Today* and *The Director Magazine* will be the route. If it is cheap holiday flights then it will be the travel section of popular magazines and newspapers.

- **Battle tanks** are of interest to just a few people in the world, so an undercover arms dealer would either phone them or arrange to meet them in an hotel in an obscure location.

■ Targeting Consumer Products

Imagine you are marketing a range of consumer products, for example a mythical range of cosmetic products that include a shampoo containing Henna extract (enriches natural red highlights in hair) and an antibacterial skin cream. They are distributed through the specialist retail trade under the brand name 'Hennderma' and sell for a higher price than supermarkets' 'own brand' equivalents.

The scenario for your initial activities may have been that you exhibited at a trade fair where wholesale and retail buyers placed orders.

Orders are are still coming in, the product is selling but you don't really know to whom and what they are doing with it. But it is important to find out as much as you can about your customers so that you can improve your marketing, focus on new product development and ensure that the advertising message appeals to the appropriate customer segment.

If you wanted additional sales of Hennderma you might for example consider direct mail or direct response advertising. But if you don't know who is buying your product, how would you start the campaign? By guessing and going ahead? Or by finding out as much as you can about your buyers (and the market place) before going ahead?

■ Who are Your Customers?

What sort of things do you need to know about your customers or users to help you to target them? A huge amount of data is available on all sections of the UK population, and this can help you to categorise and classify your buyers and potential buyers. A range of standard classifications called discriminators are commonly used in all areas of research and advertising. The more common ones are age, gender, marital state, race, geographic disposition, economic or social descriptor, lifestyle, activities.

Relevant questions are:

- Age: is your product for children, young people, the middle aged or older?

- Gender: is it a man's or a woman's product?

- Life stage: at what stage of life is it important?

- Race/religion: does race, religion or cultural grouping matter?

- Region: is the appeal of your product stronger in one part of the country than another?

In other words what type of people, defined also by economic well-being or social aspirations, will be the main users of your product or service? Using the above discriminators, the table below could define the typical user of your mythical shampoo and anti-bacterial skin cream, both of which are above average in price and quality.

	Hennderma shampoo	Hennderma antibacterial skin cream
Age	15–35	15–24
Gender	Female	Male/female
Marital state	Single/young married	Single/young married
Race	Caucasian	All types
Geographic disposition	Urban dweller	Urban dweller
Economic/social descriptor	Professional/secretarial, average income	School pupil/student/ secretarial, low income
Lifestyle	Stylish/aspirer	Follower of fashion
Activities	Likes discos, TV, cinema, magazines	Pop music, discos, sport

Apply the same descriptors to the customers and potential customers of two of your actual main products or services.

Product 1 . . . .   Product 2 . . . .

	Product 1	Product 2
Age		
Gender		
Marital state		
Race		
Geographic disposition		
Economic/social descriptor		
Lifestyle		
Activities		

■ Economic and Social Descriptors

It is important for governments and marketers to know the economic and social structure of the population. Being able to apply labels to various groups of the population facilitates this analysis.

■ Social Class

Probably the best known descriptor is social class. You may be aware of the social class definitions devised by the IPA (Independent Practitioners in Advertising) some 40 years ago and now maintained by JICNARS (The Joint Industry Council for National Audience Research). These are as follows:

Classification	Class/occupation	Percentage of the adult population
A	Upper-class captains of industry	2.6
B	Middle-class, senior executives	13.9
C 1	Lower middle class, junior execs, supervisors, senior clerical	26.8
C 2	Clerical, skilled manual	25.5
D	Manual	19.4
E	Unemployed and OAPs on state pensions only	11.8

The original idea behind the classification is that it groups together people who behave in a similar way. Because they are likely to read similar newspapers and watch similar TV programmes it allows them to be targeted through advertising. This hypothesis has stood the test of time as a very practical guide. However more sophisticated measures have been devised and used in the last decade.

What daily newspaper do you think is most likely to appeal to each of the various social classes listed above?

Social class	Newspaper
A	....
B	....
C 1	....
C 2	....
D	....
E	....

You should end up with the same newspapers for A and B. These would be *The Times, Financial Times, Independent* and *Daily Telegraph*. For C1 you will find the *Daily Mail, Daily Express* and *Guardian*. For C2 the *Mirror*. For D the *Sun* and *Sport*. For E anything you can find at the library.

There will be a fair amount of overlap, for example the *Daily Mirror* and the *Daily Mail* will claim they get as many A and B readers as *The Times*. Many C1s aspire to A or B status and will read *The Times* and the *Telegraph*. In addition the *Guardian* is read by left-wing intellectuals in groups A, B, C1 and C2.

Which social group or groups do you think are most likely to be regular buyers of Hennaderma anti-bacterial skin cream?

If you wanted to promote Hennaderma anti-bacterial skin cream through a newspaper promotion, which do you think are likely to produce the most successful results?

■ **Standard Economic Groups**

The government has always used its own classification, developed by the registrar general. The SEGs (standard economic groups) are based on professions and range from 1 (the highest) to 5 (the lowest), plus an unclassified group. The classification definitions are as follows:

Classification	Occupation	Percentage of the adult population
I	Professional occupations	4.5
II	Intermediate occupations, including most managerial and senior administrative occupations	26.3
IIIN	Skilled non manual	22.0
IIIM	Skilled manual	20.6
IV	Partly skilled occupations	15.3
V	Unskilled occupations	5.9
Other	Others	5.4

Which standard economic group, do you think are most likely to be regular buyers of Hennaderma shampoo?

```

```

■ **Census Small-Area Data**

In recent years, technology and the availability of census small-area data has led to the development of another system of socioeconomic classification.

The census, which is carried out every ten years, produces information on how many people there are in each household, their age and gender. For a 10 per cent sample the so-called census variables are calculated including measures of wealth and deprivation plus educational attainment, for example how many rooms in the house, how many cars per household, age at which education terminated and so on.

The census variables have been used to develop a system of social classification that applies to residential location, the unit being the enumeration district (ED), normally 180 households.

■ ACORN

Thus it is possible to identify on a map small units of a certain social type. The best known of these systems is a commercially developed classification called ACORN (A Classification Of Residential Neighbourhoods). This consists of 6 main, 17 subgroups and 54 sub-subgroups. The main group classifications are:

Classification	Status	Percentage of the adult population
A	Thriving	19.8
B	Expanding	11.6
C	Rising	7.5
D	Settling	24.1
E	Aspiring	13.7
F	Striving	22.8

The subdivisions are:

A	Thriving	A1	Wealthy achievers
		A2	Affluent greys
		A3	Prosperous pensioners
B	Expanding	B4	Affluent executives
		B5	Well-off workers
C	Rising	C6	Affluent urbanites
		C7	Prosperous professionals
		C8	Better-off executives
D	Settling	D9	Comfortable middle agers
		D10	Skilled workers
E	Aspiring	E11	New home owners
		E12	White-collar workers
F	Striving	F13	Older people, less prosperous areas
		F14	Council estates, better off
		F15	Council estates, high unemployment
		F16	Council estates, greatest hardship
		F17	People in multi-ethnic low-income areas

Companies that manage this type of data (called geodemographic data) can provide the following:

- An ACORN map of your marketing area.

- A list of the areas most likely to contain people who would use your type of store, facility or service.

- A list of people likely to be interested in your mail order products.

In which ACORN groups do you think the typical Hennaderma customer is likely to be?

Hennaderma shampoo

Hennaderma skin creams

Other classification systems of note are MOSAIC and PINPOINT, which do a similar job as ACORN but in a slightly different way.

■ Regional Targeting

In this chapter we have stressed the need for accurate information, not only to help you plan your marketing but also for monitoring and controlling activities such as competitor activity, sales force management or advertising campaign monitoring.

Unfortunately, directly comparable information is not always available as the various main government and private collectors and providers of consumer and business data not only use different systems, as discussed above, but also slightly different regional boundaries. This means that as part of your planning or targeting process you have to determine which criteria and which regional data to use. Be fully aware of any boundary differences, otherwise you could badly miscalculate the value of a region to your business and end up pouring expensive resources such as media budgets or valuable sales people into the wrong area.

The three main sources of regional information are the Independent Television Commission, representing the 15 independent TV companies, the Registrar General's Regions, the basis for government statistics, and A. C. Nielsen's retail audits. All three are shown on the following maps of the UK (Figures 8.3, 8.4 and 8.5). Recently postcodes have become a significant method of determining regional boundaries.

Figure 8.3   ISBA TV regions

Figure 8.4   Registrar General's regions

Figure 8.5   A.C. Nielsen regions

Various other systems have been devised by planners and researchers attempting to locate people of similar lifestyles and attitudes. Some of them are useful in certain circumstances but they are often more sophisticated than is necessary in that having identified the type of people you require there appears to be no simple way of reaching them. For example different groups of people have been described at various times as:

- Conspicuous consumers: 'Essex Man' and the recently discovered subspecies of Essex Man found only in the south-eastern part of that county – 'Lakeside Man'.

- Survivors: 'UB40 Man'.

- Self-actualisers: 'Kings Road Man'.

■ Market segmentation

■ The End of the Mass Market?

The traditional way of reaching target groups has been to use the standard classifiers. Once a company's customer research has indicated which age, gender, class and region their products will appeal to, the company then plans its advertising campaign around the media that will attract the most potential consumers in their target markets. Usually wastage is quite high, as although the customer profile may be about right, only a percentage of that profile may be interested in buying the product.

Targeting has become more important and more complex in recent years as advertising costs have soared and consumers have developed a wider range of tastes and special interests. Many of the traditional mass markets no longer exist. They have become segmented and now consist of perhaps dozens of smaller markets. For advertising to reach any of these segments cost effectively, they all need to be identified and targeted using one or more lifestyle indicators.

■ Lifestyle Indicators

Recent times have seen a new approach to the problem of market segmentation through the creation of special interest magazines. Modern technology allows the easy creation of such publications, with a subsequently rapid cessation of publishing if satisfactory performance is not achieved.

Thus people are grouped according to their interests, such as cycling, needlework, computers, food or travel. This means that targeting is made easier as people with special interests can often be reached more easily through magazines or the Internet.

Lifestyle indicators, often known as psychodemographics, combine demographic variables and activities. These include:

- Age
- Number of children
- Type and number of cars
- Credit card owners
- Business/personal travel details
- Health/fitness interests
- Collectors of antiques, pictures and so on
- Those with an interest in fine food and wine
- Hobbyists such as model railway enthusiasts

What other lifestyle indicators can you think of that would be useful to your business?

```
..................................................................................................................
..................................................................................................................
..................................................................................................................
```

Many databases exist that contain all these and many more variables and can be obtained from companies such as Mardev and Listshop.

■ Commercial and Industrial Targeting

For businesses, defining the targets is often straightforward but actually finding them can be very difficult.

■ Standard Industrial Classification

The most general classification for businesses is the SIC (Standard Industrial Classification) code. Looking at these codes is often like looking at a time warp, with many businesses only marginally classified, but recent changes to the system have made the codes more relevant for current business needs. Most commercial data bases will include the SIC code for all businesses listed.

■ Finding Your Targets

How you find your targets depends upon your type of business and the market you operate in. Using a four-digit SIC code will help you identify groups or businesses with similar activities, thus helping you to refine the accuracy of your targeting. Unfortunately there are three systems of SIC codes in use:

- Standard American, which you will find in Dunn & Bradstreet
- Pre-1992 European
- Post-1993 European

The revisions between pre- and post-1992 have made relevant changes in the industrial types listed, so industries that no longer exist have been eliminated and new industries, mainly to do with information technology, have been classified more meaningfully. The SIC code system has the following structure.

The first digit of the four digit code defines the industry:

1 Power and water industries

2 Metal extraction and other primary manufacturing

3 Other major capital goods manufacturing

4 Food, drink, tobacco and other consumables such as furniture, jewellery

5 Construction

6 Distribution and services

7 Transport

8 Services

9 Services

Combined with the first the second digit defines the industrial activity:

16 Production and distribution of electricity and gas

25 Chemicals

35 Manufacture of motor vehicles & parts

43 Textiles

61 Wholesale distribution

Finally, all four digits define the specific type of business activity:

1620 Public gas supply

2513 Fertilisers

3510 Motor vehicles

4384 Pile carpets

6170 Wholesale distribution of food

Companies such as Market Location Ltd will provide you with a full SIC listing, including a count of their file entries for each SIC subcode.

■ An Industrial Targeting Exercise

You have just been appointed as the marketing manager of a small engineering company (employing 40 people), which for twenty years has specialised in working with spring steel. It has the equipment to make coil springs of all sizes from 6 mm in diameter to 200 mm in diameter. It also produces spring steel strip to any size and can make any similar products using spring steel that their customers might want.

Your MD wants a brief report on current and future marketing activities. What do you think the company's markets are? (Its SIC code is 3138: heat and surface treatment of metals. 31 = manufacture of metal goods.)

```
..........................................................................................
..........................................................................................
```

What types of customer does it target at present?

```
..........................................................................................
..........................................................................................
```

Considering its specialist skills, are there any new customer types it could target?

```
..........................................................................................
..........................................................................................
```

Did you try the exercise? Perhaps you thought 'I'm not interested in industrial products like that'. OK, but you should be doing a similar exercise for your own market.

■ Where is Your Target Market?

Again how you find your targets depends upon your type of business and the market you operate in. The customers of a retail establishment may all live within half a mile of or within the town, or they may be scattered throughout the county.

Do you know who they are or where they live? Clearly if your shop sells substantial items on credit, or items that need to be delivered, such as furniture, then the names and addresses of customers will be to hand for analysis, but if it is a baker or a grocer then it is probable that customers' names and addresses will not be available and some kind of research will be required to establish the shop's catchment area.

Completing the following table will help you define the market or users for each of your products or services.

Product/service	Description of current users

Now consider the question: what type of potential is there for you that you are not exploiting?

Complete the following target market table by defining potential new customers for each of your products or services.

Product/service	Description of target market/customers
. . . .	. . . .
. . . .	. . . .
. . . .	. . . .
. . . .	. . . .
. . . .	. . . .
. . . .	. . . .

Pricing for the Market: Pricing Policy

'How do I know what's the right price to charge for my product or service?' This is one of the questions most often asked – but one which frequently remains unanswered!

Everything put into your marketing plan, all the interrelated components of the marketing mix for each product or service you offer, all the creative advertising you can muster, all of the packaging – ultimately depend on the price you set.

Too high and overall returns diminish as buyers disappear and volumes fall. Too low and larger than expected volumes are required to generate sufficient returns, or even worse, volumes fall creating pressure on margins because buyers consider the product to be too cheap.

Get it right and the volume and contribution is as you expect, but more importantly the buyer is satisfied and having a satisfied customer is the first step towards developing a long-term relationship with that customer. Getting it right means understanding the markets you operate in and knowing at what price potential buyers will choose your product rather than a competitor's product.

■ Cost Plus Pricing

Even today too many businesses use cost plus as the basis for pricing their goods or services. They still expect their estimating or costing department to add together the four elements of product costing – materials, direct labour, allocated overheads and a percentage for profit – and use the result as the sole determinant of the market price for their products or services.

Sometimes, especially during boom periods or seasonal peaks, the cost plus formula works very well as strong enquiry levels help develop an acceptable

99

level of sales and operating profits. Problems tend to arise when competitor pressure increases or the market turns down, creating an oversupply of their particular product or service. Then these cost plus businesses wonder why they are not only losing business to their competitors but are also having to discount more and more to retain what's left.

As you will have realised when you completed the price element of the marketing mix matrix in Chapter 5, pricing is a key element of virtually every marketing mix, but pricing without referring to the market place is usually nothing more than 'cost plus guestimating'. This means that product or service costings are calculated from the 'bottom up' by adding together the component parts and then adding an operating or profit margin. The result is the price at which the business would like to sell its product or service, that is:

Materials + direct labour + overheads + margin = selling price

But cost plus only provides part of the price equation, the price that the business would like to receive for its products or services. The market place determines the remainder – the price buyers consider acceptable for that item.

In order to develop a successful pricing policy that is consistently in tune with the market, product pricing should be approached from the 'top down', what the market expects to pay; not just from the 'bottom up', to suit the businesses needs. The 'top down' or market-led approach to pricing puts the buyer's price expectations before the cost plus expectations of the seller:

Market price – materials – direct labour – overheads = contribution margin

Price should not now be a stumbling block for sales, and providing the contribution margin is sufficient or in accord with other business objectives, then the price established is now acceptable to both buyer and seller:

The acceptable price = buyer acceptance + satisfactory margin

If, however, the forecast contribution is not considered acceptable, then either all the other costs will have to be reviewed downwards or consideration will have to be given to withdrawing that product or service from that particular market.

To summarise the points covered so far for pricing policy, see Figure 9.1.

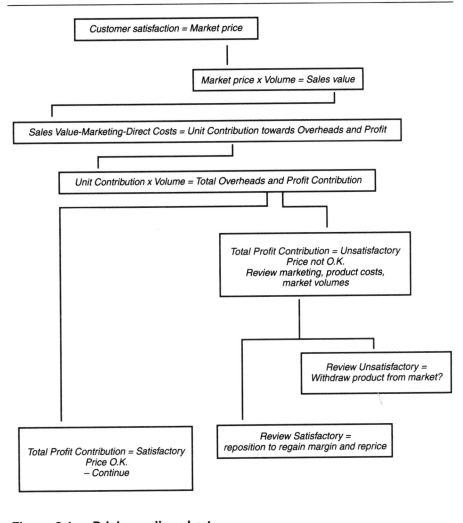

Figure 9.1   Pricing policy chart

■ Cost Plus and Plus

This is the point where cost plus pricing fails so many businesses, especially subcontractors providing products or services in industries such as engineering or construction. What tends to happen is that as their markets weaken and supply exceeds demand, their buyer's price expectations become lower, making the unchanging cost plus pricing of the subcontractor too high. The subcontractor starts to lose contracts and as a result revenues and contributions fall, but as operating costs often remain the same the business now needs cost plus and an additional margin just to maintain profit expectations – 'cost plus and plus'.

The alternative strategy that many businesses in this position adopt is to continue pricing on a cost plus basis but then reduce just the estimated profit margin in order to secure the work they now desperately need. The resulting price often leaves very little profit on the contract, and usually no profit at all or an operating loss if anything goes wrong. Continuing this pricing policy for any length of time means that many of these businesses will start to incur operating losses that in some cases will become unsustainable, and in time these business will fail.

■ Determining the Acceptable Price Band

Whilst each of the four main cost elements discussed above is vital when determining the costs involved, the development of a profitable pricing policy in any competitive market place can only be achieved if there is a clear understanding of the way the market works, the main competitors operating in it and the price band or price range perceived by the buyer as acceptable value for money for a particular product (Figure 9.2).

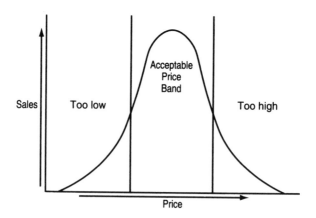

Figure 9.2   The acceptable price band

However there is not often just one price at which a product will sell. Consumers and professional buyers are continuously evaluating products and services they are interested in buying. As a result, unless a product or service is new to the market or totally unique, every consumer, buyer or user develops a mental or written price range within which any item under consideration is perceived to be value for money. In developing this price range not only are immediate competitors considered, but also the value of any substitutes that could be used instead.

If the price is above this perceived range then the supplier needs to provide strong justification of the higher price in order to secure a sale; if on the other hand the price is below the accepted range then this presents the supplier with the difficulty of persuading buyers that they are getting a bargain and not just an inferior product. (Too low a price can often be a negative influence on sales volumes.)

How do you determine the key components of your pricing policy? What is the acceptable price range for your product or service?

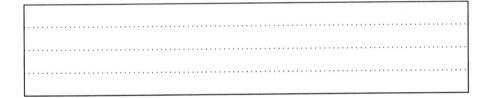

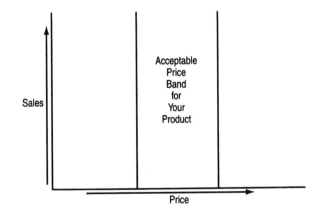

Figure 9.3   The acceptable price band for your product

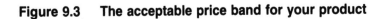

Where buyers situate each product on their own price–value scale depends on a variety of factors, not least of which is each producer's marketing efforts, because as often as not all products in the value range are compared but the cheapest is not necessarily chosen. The marketing of the higher-value product helps to dissuade the buyer from choosing solely according to price by highlighting non-price factors such as quality, style, taste, packaging and so on.

Once the producer has identified the upper and lower limits of the perceived price band for products similar to the one to be priced, the next stage is to evaluate the main competing products, their prices (published and unpublished), the competitors' marketing activities and their sales volumes. This information can be used to produce an estimate of the size and value of the market segment under scrutiny.

Taking into account all the other elements of the marketing mix, a new product – or one requiring repositioning – can now positioned within its market segment and priced accordingly. Do you have sufficient information to price or reprice your products or services within their price bands?

Yes ☐   No ☐

If you have answered 'no' to the above question make a list of the information you require:

■ Product Repositioning

Following the basic steps outlined above is crucial for all those pricing or repricing products. Unit margins may appear wonderful at the top end of your market but there is little point in trying to develop or reposition a product to take advantage of these margins if the resulting volumes sold are not sufficient to keep your machinery or workforce efficiently employed.

A profitable pricing policy firstly identifies the acceptable price range for the product or service, then – using this price band as the starting point – considers the volumes that can be achieved and – after deducting direct materials and labour – the margin left for a contribution towards overheads and profit.

Changes to the product marketing mix can help differentiate a product from its competitors and reposition it within this price band, or even move it up or down to another. These changes, including price changes, will increase or decrease the number of units sold and the overall forecast product contribution. In most established markets these changes are unlikely to affect the total sales of that price band, unless the product is a very dominant brand leader or that market segment is particularly sensitive to price changes.

> If the unit margin (considered in this case to be the overall contribution after marketing costs) and the forecast volume of sales are acceptable, then the price has been established – for the present.

If any of the above factors are not acceptable and there is no question of bringing about an improvement by reducing the direct costs or reevaluating the marketing mix, then it is time to think about dropping that product or withdrawing from that particular market.

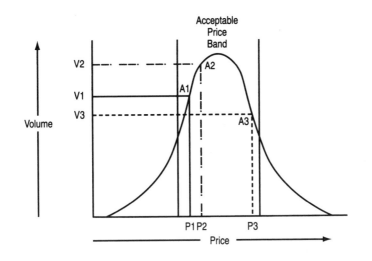

Figure 9.4   The acceptable price band (repositioning)

In Figure 9.4 a product priced at position (A1) is repositioned within its acceptable price band to position (A2) at a higher price (P2). This price increase is achieved by adjusting the product's marketing mix, packaging, advertising and so on. The result is that not only is the product accepted at the higher price (P2) but also – because of the better positioning – there is an increase in the total volume sold (V2). Provided that the extra contribution from the new level of sales exceeds the additional marketing costs, then the product will generate higher profits than before. However had the decision been to position the product even higher up the perceived price–quality range to (A3), then although unit margins would have been higher at price (P3), volume sales (V3) would have been lower than the the levels achieved before the repositioning commenced.

■ Intangible Products and Services

Buyers of intangible products such as financial plans or holidays can be expected to react in a similar fashion to that described above, so producers and sellers of these products can determine the market price of their products in a similar way.

■ Relationship Pricing

We have already shown that the cost plus or cost accounting approach to product pricing is archaic and inaccurate. Adopting a marketing-led pricing policy means understanding, implementing and developing the concept of relationship pricing. Relationship pricing simply means establishing your prices in relation to:

- The price range that buyers consider acceptable (back to the bell curve).

- The price range over which your competitors are selling similar products.

The buyer's value-for-money price band can move up and down the value scale for a variety of reasons, such as increases or decreases in confidence or seasonal changes, and as a result pricing policy needs to be constantly reviewed in order to ensure not only that the price remains stable in relation to that of its competitor, but also that the position within the potential buyer's perceived price range has not changed. Many businesses allocate so much of their marketing effort to watching their competitors that they often fail to notice changes in customer behaviour until it is too late. Conversely other businesses expend much of their effort on customer watching, and as a result aggressive competitor activity catches them unaware.

In a stable market it is important to maintain these two relationships in equilibrium in order to maintain volume and contribution and to ensure that if they move, they move together and in the same direction. If efforts are being made to improve the product's overall position through an adjustment of its marketing mix that is, by repackaging, altering the product image or adding value in some other way – the change in these relationships needs to be forecast beforehand and continuously monitored afterwards to ensure that the repositioning has proceeded as planned.

Adopting the concept of relationship pricing means there is no longer any need to price blindfolded or stab in the dark. Pricing becomes a proactive element of marketing instead of a reactive, defensive measure and should result in:

- More knowledgeable and increasingly confident managers.

- Better margins.

- More accurate financial planning.

- Less chance of being involved in a price war, unless you start it!

And perhaps most importantly of all:

- More satisfied customers.

A satisfied customer is more likely to return to you in the future, either to buy the same product or service again or to buy others you provide. You only have to consider how much each customer could spend on your products or services over the next five or ten years – *the life-time value of the customer* – in order to realise how much extra revenue and profit could be generated in the future by adopting a relationship pricing policy.

■ Subcontractors and Other Business-to-Business Services

Unlike the butcher, the baker or the vehicle manufacturer, a great many businesses do not have distinct products or services to package and sell. Construction subcontractors, component suppliers, software programmers, printers and many others have to prepare new bills of quantities, work programmes or production schedules every time an enquiry is received.

'Main contractors buy on price only' is the most usual comment by the owners and managers of the large proportion of subcontracting and other service businesses who believe that – because of a combination of the competitive and often aggressive nature of their customers (who are always telling them that their prices are too high) and because every estimate they produce is different – pricing for the market does not apply to them.

Most of these businesses leave pricing to their estimating department, which invariably uses the 'cost plus' method of pricing when preparing an estimate. As we have already seen, this is just one half of the pricing equation.

Many directors and sales managers admit that they only review a small proportion of the estimates prepared in this way before they are sent out, and those tend to be just the larger ones or those where they have a personal involvement. This means that, in these businesses, the majority of estimates are prepared and sent out without referring to anyone who has responsibility for evaluating the market price. Does this happen in your business?

Yes    No

As this is common practice in most businesses that prepare individual quotations, it means that a major proportion of all estimates, quotations and tenders sent to buyers are not much more than 'guestimates', and as such most are probably discarded as soon as they are received as being too far removed from the contract price range to be worth considering further. How many of the estimates or quotations submitted by your business or organisation end up this way?

Cost plus pricing through the estimating department without reference to the current market price can produce haphazard results, as the following example illustrates.

A previously profitable, medium-sized subcontracting business began to lose money but did not know why. As part of the process of identifying what was going wrong, all the estimates prepared over the previous twelve months were analysed. This revealed that in general the business was winning a high percentage of the smaller contracts it quoted for but was losing most of the large ones. The reason for this turned out to be quite simple. The estimating department had always added a standard percentage margin when pricing.

When times were good the firm's estimate prices were competitive and the value of contracts won was more evenly spread. But as the market declined contract prices dropped and competitors who had abandonded fixed percentage estimating in favour of evaluating the overall contract contribution started to win a larger proportion of the bigger contracts. This left the 'cost plus' business with a reduced turnover and a high proportion of smaller contracts, each returning the desired percentage margin but each with an insufficient 'actual' gross profit to enable the business to make an operating profit. Those responsible said they had always been 'too busy' to complete contract profit evaluations. Because of this, until business declined they had not realised that most of their smaller contracts had never made sufficient profit to cover their costs.

The business revised its pricing procedure and, amongst other changes, introduced the second half of the price equation – identifying the price range for each contract. The first effect of this new policy was an overall increase in the estimate price for the smaller contracts, which produced a substantial increase in the profitability of these contracts with very little loss of volume, a clear indication that these contracts had been underpriced in the past. The second effect was an overall decrease in the margin on larger work as contracts were priced closer to the current market price. The increased number of large contracts won quickly compensated for the lower unit profitability and the business returned to profit within a few months.

■ Estimating the Market Price

Contrary to the view frequently expressed, market pricing can take place in an industrial subcontracting or business service environment. It may not be as easy as for those businesses with ready access to details of their competitors' prices and other information, but the philosophy is the same and the techniques are very similar. It requires a slightly different approach, a little more effort and the addition of something lacked by many subcontracting businesses, both large and small – someone to take control of and be responsible for the implementation of all elements of marketing for the business.

In order to successfully introduce effective market pricing into any businesses, some new techniques may need to be learnt and understood, and a number of simple procedures implemented and controlled. In addition it is important to ensure that the concepts of marketing and market pricing are accepted by all those involved. Some of the most important techniques and procedures needed to develop a market-led pricing policy are outlined below.

■ Identify the Industry Cycle

Most subcontracting businesses are not big enough or dominant enough in their particular industry to become price setters, and it is the volume of work obtained by their main contractors that tends to have the greatest effect on the prices they can obtain.

Profitable pricing can take place during downswings of a business cycle as well as upturns. So the first step for a subcontractor who wants to improve sales levels and profits by pricing for the market is to determine where on the business cycle the contractor's industry is likely to be in order to identify what is likely to be the most profitable price range to quote within.

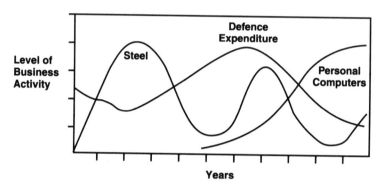

Figure 9.5   Typical industry cycles

Regular increases and decreases in output or sales can be recorded for most industrial and business-to-business sectors. These changes in the business cycle may be seasonal or spread over a number of years. Plotted over a period of time, a regular cycle – or wavelength – of change can usually be identified. During downturns in this cycle contract prices and profits are reduced as the volume of work falls away and gradually increase as demand returns at the begining of the next cycle.

Knowing the wavelength of previous cycles, peak to peak or trough to trough, is one of the first steps towards determining where on the business cycle your main contractor's industry is likely to be in order to identify the most profitable price range to quote within. If you can achieve this you will discover that profitable pricing can take place during downswings of a business cycle as well as upturns.

This is not as difficult as it sounds as the most important aspect of profitable pricing – market knowledge, the missing part of the pricing equation – is readily available. In every business there is a substantial pool of knowledge and data relating to products, customers, markets and competitors. The problem is usually that it is stored in people's heads, old filing cabinets or archived records.

■ Use Marketing Activities to Help Counter Price-Driven Competitors

It has been shown that offering the lowest price is not necessarily the only way to win a contract. A range of marketing techniques can be used to help, develop the other elements of your marketing mix to counter price-driven competition.

What non-price factors could you use to counter the objection 'I would like to give you the job but you're not the cheapest'?

```
..................................................................................
..................................................................................
..................................................................................
..................................................................................
..................................................................................
```

Who wants to do business with the cheapest if they are unreliable and the work is urgent? Use recommendations and testimonials to show existing and potential customers how reliable your business is. An agreed level of product reliability or service quality will be expected from you – what happens to the supplier who consistently fails to keep to these agreed standards?

Most of the British contracting industry now considers that quality and reliability are more important than price alone. Offer your customers a package of satisfaction that includes these factors as well as a price that is acceptable to both of you and you will not only win more contracts than your cost-plus competitors, but also start to develop the type of long-term business relationships that enables a business to prosper and grow!

CHAPTER 10

Market Planning: Forecasting

In this chapter we will explain some of the techniques used when forecasting, how to use the Boston Matrix as an analytical tool to aid decision making and – once you have prepared your forecasts – how to identify the key monitors that will help you keep on track.

■ What Do You Want to Predict?

Forecasting is an attempt to avoid problems of over- or under-investing. Clearly you want to be able to forecast your net profit, but this of course is entirely dependent on diverse activities in the business that can have contradictory effects. Most businesses set out to forecast sales units or cash, and then calculate other data from these.

The simplest form of forecasting is to look at the apparent extension of the sales trend. The starting point is to look at the sales graph and see whether a simple trend is indicated. This is known as a time series. A ruler will often tell you a lot without having to resort to complex mathematical routines. The mathematical equivalent of the ruler is linear regression, which looks complicated but in principle is very simple – you do need to know some algebra however!

> In years gone by farmers would fatten the occasional pig for market. Not knowing how to calculate the weight and therefore the value of their porker they would cajole it onto one side of a crudely constructed balance scale. On the other side of the scale they piled boulders and stones until the two balanced. Then they guessed the weight of the stones!

There are number of technical points to take into account when forecasting, including:

- Seasonality: we all know that sales peak for some items at different times of the year, and sales of items may peak at different times of the week, for example at weekends.

- Trends: is your market increasing, decreasing or static? Are your customer age groups getting younger, older or staying the same? Is this year's main colour green, yellow, blue or taupe? All these should be borne in mind when finalising your forecast.

Initially you need to prepare a sales forecast based on sales history. When a simple sales forecast is being prepared using historical sales figures as the base, it is necessary to separate the two elements in the data: seasonality and trend.

■ Seasonality

In most cases the seasonality of sales data follows the calendar. Peaks occur at different times of the year because of social and meteorological causes. Here are some illustrative examples in UK markets.

- Toy sales peak in November and December.

- Food sales peak in late December and just before Easter (some time between late March and late April).

- Holiday sales peak in January (although actual holiday taking peaks in late July through August).

- Spirit sales peak in December.

- Beer sales peak in July and August and again in late December.

Some of these peaks are huge, accounting for over 70 per cent of sales. In others the peaks are substantial but not quite as dominant.

■ Trends

In order to see which way sales are moving overall there is a need to look at the trends in the data. At the end of the year you can determine which way the trends are heading by comparing your annual sales with those of the previous year. However this will be too slow a process for some, so to help you keep an eye on the trend the data can be deseasonalised by taking the average of the twelve-month sales up to and including the month being deseasonalised. Having reduced the range of variation by removing the seasonality it is much easier to observe the sales trend.

NB: If you are observing a money series over a period of several years you will need to consider indexing the data to eliminate the effect of inflation.

The following example uses data from a small business (Company A) operating in the leisure industry. The actual monthly sales range between £2000 and £9500 whereas the deseasonalised monthly sales range between £5000 and £6500. The monthly sales pattern is plotted out.

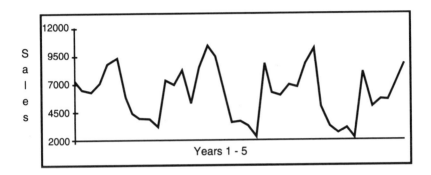

Figure 10.1 Monthly sales

To understand what is happening we need to separate out the recurring seasonality to see where the trend line is leading. The data can be deseasonalised by use of the moving annual average or total (Figure 10.2).

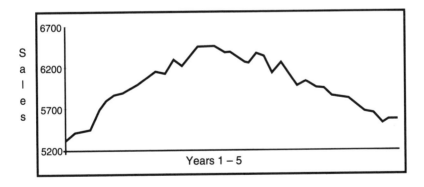

Figure 10.2 Deseasonalised monthly sales

In principle the deseasonalised sale in month (n) is the sum (S) of months $n-11$ to month n divided by 12. This can be expressed algebraically as:

$$\sum (Sm)/12m = n - 11, n$$

Most experts believe that a seasonal calculation that takes the average right in the middle of the series is the best representation, but for practical purposes it has disadvantages in that you have to wait six months to get the relevant data to tell where your trend line is going.

Many computer programs are available today that will forecast future sales trends. If data on just the first eighteen months had been available then the computer program would have selected a straight line heading upwards towards a £7000 per month average within six months.

■ **Forecasting Sales Using Linear Regression (Figure 10.3)**

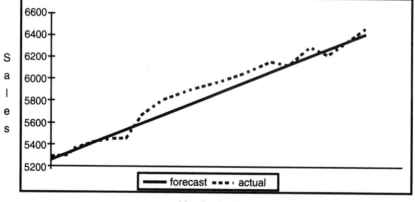

Months 1–18

Figure 10.3   Forecast and actual sales (linear)

Linear regression is the method of least squares. That is, the sum of the squares of the deviations from the filled line is less than from any other line.

However, analysis of data covering four years indicates that a linear model is inappropriate. Indeed the computer program would have selected a curved line, which in this case is a quadratic curve.

■ **Forecasting Sales Using Multiple Regression (Figure 10.4)**

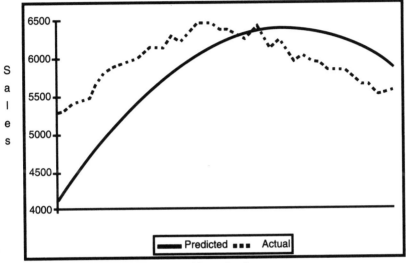

Years 2 – 5

Figure 10.4 Forecast and actual sales (regression)

Whilst the sales data alone would not have predicted what actually happened in years three and four, observing what was happening in the prevailing economy would have aided more accurate forecasting. Many industries react to major changes in the economy some time after the changes have taken place. It is important to be aware of the economic lag that applies in your market.

■ **Logistic and Gompertz Curves**

It is unlikely that the sales trend for any business or product will be a straight line, although it may be over a short period. Deseasonalised sales data often follow fairly classical curves, such as the logistic and Gompertz curves illustrated here (Figures 10.5 and 10.6).

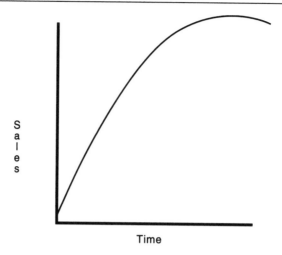

Figure 10.5   Logistic curve

These curves represent the theoretical growth patterns of biological populations but sales of new products tend to grow in the same way, thus the same principles can be used to predict sales trends.

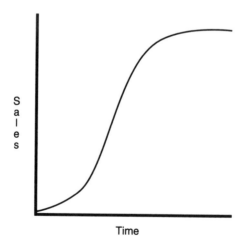

Figure 10.6   Gompertz curve

Most computer spreadsheet programs have a curve-fitting facility so you can easily test how your sales are growing (or not!) Care should be taken to check that the results are sensible. Your computer model will produce statistics to tell you whether the curve produced is a reasonable fit or not, or indeed whether the data is behaving in a predictable way.

■ Planning Scenarios

The next layer above time series is a mathematical model in which the dependent variable – for example sales or market size – is calculated from a relationship that includes other variables. These models are useful in developing planning scenarios such as:

● If interest rates drop and unemployment falls what level of house-building will there be?

● If next week is hot, how much ice-cream will be eaten?

● If we have a hot summer and the economy picks up, how many people will visit your part of the country?

By examining past data and using regression techniques it is possible to build such predictive models. Clearly they are dependent upon the accuracy of the measured values of the predictor variables and the models suffer if too many predictors are involved, and in some cases you are merely substituting one guess for another. To help improve your forecasting we have included historical data on some common economic variables at the end of this chapter.

■ Economic Market Models

However market forecasting using models based on economic indicators is very popular and organisations such as the Henley Centre, EIU and LBS and most major banks provide forecasts of future economic activity.

It may be that you are a supplier to just one other company, in which case your forecasting should be strongly related to what that customer is going to do. In this case a face-to-face meeting on the subject will get you most of the way there.

If you are responsible for forecasting your sales, remember that someone has to achieve these sales. Breaking down or building up the sales by customer or salesman can be quite salutary: 'You want me to sell *how much!* I've only got *five* customers and *two* of those are dead!' You need to understand any limiting factors that might prevent your forecasts from being achieved.

■ The Product Life Cycle

It is believed that all products go through a life cycle that has four main phases:

- Initiation
- Growth
- Maturity
- Decline

A classic product life-cycle curve illustrating the relationship of each of these four phases is shown below.

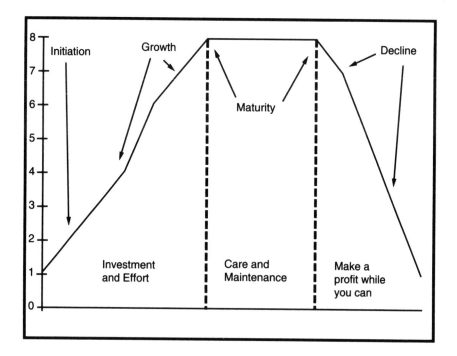

Figure 10.7   Product life cycle

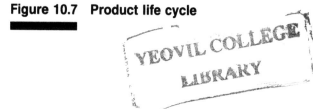

You need to decide what phase you are in as this directs the marketing of your product or service. The initiation and growth stages need investment, above-average advertising and effort. The mature stage needs maintenance – that is, money and care – and the decline needs milking (do not even give them free carrier bags!)

Perhaps you can think of some markets and products in these various stages. Sometimes it is difficult to know what stage you are in and it is dangerous to act hastily.

Consider the following example of Product X. The product life-cycle charts in Figures 10.8, 10.9 and 10.10 are for a well-known consumer product that was introduced in 1953. Years 1–12 clearly show the introduction and initial growth stages of the life cycle and the maturity stage extends through to its seventeenth year.

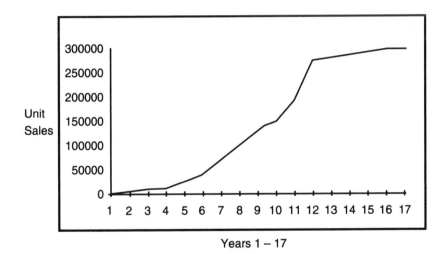

Years 1 – 17

Figure 10.8   Product X: years 1–17

Clearly in year 17 the product was on a plateau and the company could only predict static sales or decline. But changes in marketing produced spectacular growth over the next ten years and unit sales of the brand trebled.

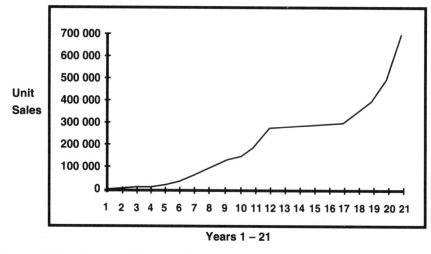

Figure 10.9   Product X: years 1–21

A somewhat chastened forecaster asked to predict the next ten years would probably have predicted rather less growth than actually occurred. The changes in the sales pattern did not happen spontaneously – they were the result of deliberate policy changes in marketing, which paid off with continually increasing sales of what is today one of the world's leading consumer brands.

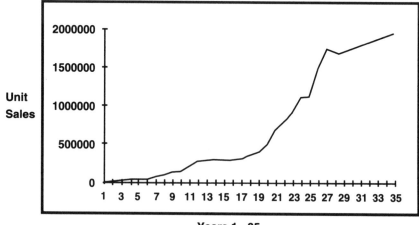

Figure 10.10   Product X: years 1–35

■ Growth, Maturity or Decline?

Of course many products have an obvious life cycle. The end comes for valid reasons, but many brands or products can be repackaged, repositioned and revitalised.

Beechams is a company that does not believe in letting its brands die – look what it has done with Lucozade, Ribena and Horlicks. Lucozade was once marketed as the recuperative drink for invalids but it is now promoted as an athlete's post-performance restorative. Ribena was a blackcurrant concentrate your mother gave you because it had lots of vitamin C, now it comes carbonated in a can. Horlicks was a late-night drink that helped you sleep but now it is advertised as a low-fat health drink to help you relax.

Likewise Unilever's Persil has a long history and has gone through many changes in formulation and packaging; the same applies to Procter & Gamble's Fairy soap and washing-up liquid.

On the other hand we could produce a long list of products and brands that are no longer with us. As an exercise, see how many products and brands you can list that have died in the last ten years and how many you know that have been revitalised.

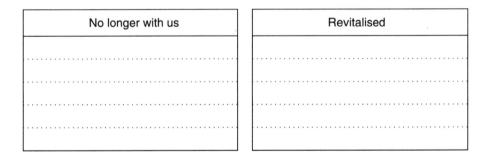

No longer with us	Revitalised

Most products that disappear do so because they have become technologically redundant. The typewriter replaced the pen in offices and now word processors and e-mail are replacing the typewriter. 100 years ago if you had asked one of your staff to make a copy of a 50-page document they would have disappeared for a month – now they just trip along to the photocopier for five minutes or set their word processor to print as many copies as required.

Some products almost disappear but then come back. Formerly in the UK many people travelled on bicycles, but greater wealth and the boom in car ownership has led to a steady decline in adult bicycle purchases. Now their use for urban commuting and leisure has resulted in a tremendous sales revival.

Are your products or service at the growth, mature or decline stage? If they are in decline can you do something about it?

Product	Life-cycle stage	Action

■ The Boston Matrix

The Boston Matrix is a useful analytical tool that can be used in many situations and in principle has four states, as shown in Figure 10.11. Before you finally decide on what action to take with your products consider their position on this matrix.

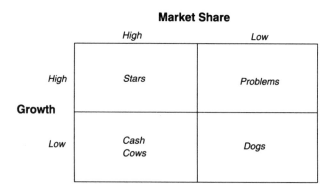

Figure 10.11   The Boston matrix

- If you have a high share in a high-growth market you've got a *Star* – the world is your oyster.

- If you have a high share in a low-growth (possibly declining) market the product is a *Cash Cow*. Get what profit you can from it – don't invest.

- If you have a low share in a high-growth market it is worth doing something to get a better share – you have a *Problem* to solve.

- If you have a low share in a low-growth market the product is a *Dog* – forget it.

Which of your products are Stars, which are Problems and which are Dogs? Hopefully you have some Cash Cows too!

Product/service	Status (Star, Cash Cow, Problem, Dogs)

Using this analytical technique will enable you to judge how to market your product or service.

■ Key Monitors

Once you have developed your forecasts you need to check progress against forecasts – to see:

- If you are on course.

- If something is going wrong (under- or over- achievement).

Our view is that most businesses can be managed from information summaries contained on one sheet of A4 paper. These key monitors can be worth their weight in gold to the busy manager provided that:

- The information is relevant.

- The information is accurate.

- The information is current.

- All the primary data from which the information summary has been prepared is quickly and easily accessible in the event of a query.

Computerisation means that a mass of data is readily available, but often it is too detailed to absorb easily and frequently it is in a report format that suits the data user rather than the decision maker. For example full listings of aged creditors or debtors may suit accounts, but usually all the decision maker needs is the totals. This can mean that information is not available when required or normal work is disrupted in order to produce one or two important statistics.

However it is necessary to have sufficient financial and other management information in order to be able to make effective decisions based on knowledge of all the relevant facts. Therefore there is a need to establish a range of key indicators that can each provide a measure of the performance of a particular aspect of the business.

Each business has different needs, pressures and long-term objectives and it is up to individual managers to develop a range of key monitors they are comfortable with and that provide them with the information they need. Key data should be recorded, reported and collated regularly and the monitors calculated on a daily, weekly, monthly or quarterly basis, depending on the figures, their application and the type of business involved.

Figures by themselves are often meaningless, and to be of most benefit the actual statistics produced should be compared with the original forecasts for the period. For each set of data to be monitored it is necessary to establish variances, or tolerance levels, from the original forecast. Within the tolerance range deviation from the forecast is acceptable, but as soon as a figure moves outside its agreed range then this should be noted, investigated and, if necessary, corrective action taken.

Together these indicators can provide a fairly accurate snapshot of overall performance and can be particularly useful when used as a supplement to monthly or quarterly management accounts. If all the information collected is maintained in a standard format, preferably on one page, then any variation from the norm in any area of the business can immediately be identified and investigated.

Some of the main statistics or activities it would be beneficial to monitor are listed in the table below. Consider what factors you need to monitor in your business. Are they different from those in the table? If so add them to the activity list at the end of this chapter.

For each item determine the maximum variation from the norm or from established targets that would be tolerable and enter this figure in the appropriate box (usually expressed as +/− per cent of the forecast or target). Now for each item listed decide the likely outcome if the variance is exceeded, either over or under, and what course of action, if any, you need to take. Remember that the items you choose as your key monitors need not only be financial information. They could also relate to other activities that affect your forecast variations, such as the level of sales enquiries, quality standards or productivity. Do not forget that in some circumstances overachievement can cause problems, such as overtrading, stock and materials shortages or administrative bottlenecks, and sometimes dissatisfied customers!

What are your key activities and what percentage variation against forecast can you tolerate and expect?

Figure 10.12 is an example of a key monitor form and shows some of the important areas that need to be monitored by the marketing manager of a manufacturing company with a field salesforce selling a heavily advertised new product to the retail trade. Sales are above forecast – bonuses all round! But our key monitors are showing disturbing variances and if these are part of a trend, profitability is rapidly being eroded – trouble is looming instead!

Daily ☐

Weekly ☐

Monthly ☐

Activity Level   Period

	Forecast	Actual	Difference (+/-%)	Maximum allowance Variance from Forecast (+/-%)	Comments or actions
Enquiries this period	300	270	-10%	+/-5%	Investigate
Sales this period	60	62	+5%	+/-2%	Great!
Advertising expenditure	£1500	£2000	+33%	+10%	Cost breakdown required
Cost per enquiry	£5	£7.4	+48%	+/-5%	Review ads & schedule
Cost per sale	£25	£32.25	+29%	+/-3%	How much!
Enquiry/sales ratio	1:5	1:4	+20%	+/-5%	Not the sales team's fault!

Other key monitors could include

Total sales by type; – by salesman – by area – by type of product – by division, retail, trade, commercial Enquiries by salesman Factory order book value – by type of customer Order dispatch lead time – Retail Overtime this period Quantity of items produced per man (40hrs) (monthly only)	Financial Monitors Invoiced value this period – by retail – by trade Total debtors by type: Retail, Trade, Commerce, Other Aged Debtors Total Creditors Bank borrowings Stock levels/value (quarterly only) Any unbudgeted expenditure

Figure 10.12   Key monitors

■ Key Monitor Charts

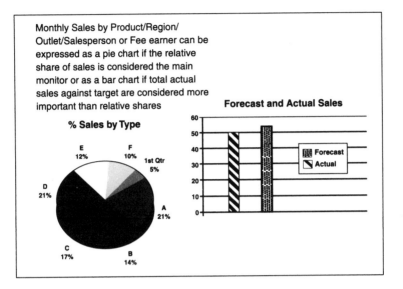

Monthly Sales by Product/Region/ Outlet/Salesperson or Fee earner can be expressed as a pie chart if the relative share of sales is considered the main monitor or as a bar chart if total actual sales against target are considered more important than relative shares

% Sales by Type

Forecast and Actual Sales

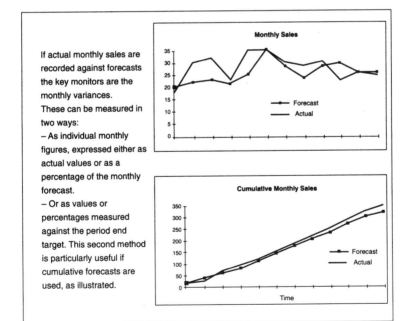

If actual monthly sales are recorded against forecasts the key monitors are the monthly variances.
These can be measured in two ways:
– As individual monthly figures, expressed either as actual values or as a percentage of the monthly forecast.
– Or as values or percentages measured against the period end target. This second method is particularly useful if cumulative forecasts are used, as illustrated.

Figure 10.13　Key monitor charts

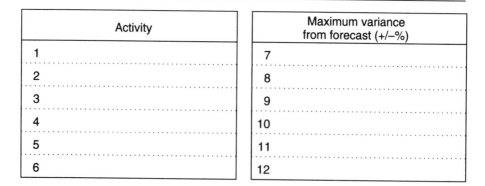

Activity		Maximum variance from forecast (+/–%)	
1		7	
2		8	
3		9	
4		10	
5		11	
6		12	

■ External Variables

Earlier in the chapter we discussed external influences that could affect your plan. The time series in Figure 10.14 shows historic data of two important financial series: interest rates and retail price inflation. Can you forecast the changes that are likely to occur over the next few years?

This information is readily available in the CSO's *Monthly Digest of Statistics* and publications such as the *Financial Times*.

Year	1980	81	82	83	84	85	86	87	88	89	90	91	92	93	94	95	96	*97*	*98*	*99*
Base rate	12	17	11	9	14	12	11	8	12	15	14	10	6	5	6	6	6	*8*	*8*	*9*
RPI	14	12	5	5	7	6	4	5	7	7	10	5	3	2	2	3	3	*5*	*6*	*7*

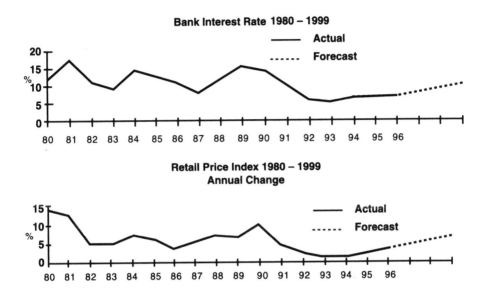

Figure 10.14   Bank interest rates and retail price index

CHAPTER 11

Marketing Communication: Sending the Message

■ The Medium is More Important than the Message

Good products or good ideas will probably fail if you talk to the wall! No matter how creative your advertising is or how good your proposition, if you cannot transmit your message to the right target audience your campaign is likely to be ineffectual and a high proportion of the budget will be wasted. Therefore, now that we know who or what we are trying to reach as our target we must decide how to communicate with them, and what to say.

Marketing communications is a term used to encompass every aspect of the visual, written, spoken or sensory interaction between a business and its market(s). The avenues of communication can include public relations, publicity, editorial coverage, media advertising, shop frontages and point-of-sale display. Your plan might just concentrate on one avenue or several in order to help develop a balanced and cost-effective promotional mix.

Whatever the communication avenue or avenues you choose to use, the following ten-point plan will help improve the effectiveness of your campaign.

■ Planning an Advertising Campaign

The main ingredients of a successful campaign are:

- Targeting
- Planning

- Media selection
- Creativity

Within our ten-point plan, these ingredients should be considered in the following order:

- Determine the objectives of the campaign.
- Determine the target audience.
- Determine the communication avenues.
- Determine timing and seasonality.
- Select the target segment.
- Select the media.
- Prepare the plan.
- List the product benefits.
- Prepare the message.
- Launch the campaign.

In order to understand how this process can benefit your advertising planning, complete the following exercise.

■ Determine the Objectives of the Campaign

What do you want to achieve?

- To sell?
- To communicate a new concept?
- To raise awareness of company or product?

What are your campaign objectives?

```
..............................................................................
..............................................................................
..............................................................................
..............................................................................
```

■ Determine your target audience

Who do you want to talk to?

- Customers?
- Potential customers?
- Influencers?

What is your main target audience and how many are there in each group?

Group	Group size
....	....
....	....
....	....

■ Determine Your Media Options

What is the most effective way of delivering the message?

- PR: editorial?
- Media advertising: TV, radio, newspapers, magazines, display, classified?
- Direct mail?

What are your media options?

....
....
....

As well as more conventional media – that is, press, television and radio – it may be appropriate for you to use local poster sites (excellent if you have a store and there is passing trade) or mobile poster sites (backs or sides of buses and taxis or your own vehicles).

For business to business, direct mail by SIC code to the right type of business may be more appropriate. Direct mail can also work well for certain consumer groups that are not highly concentrated but can be reached through special mailing-house lists.

■ **Determine any Timing or Seasonality Factors that could Influence the Response**

What timing factors could affect your plan?

Is the time of week important?   Yes [   ]   No [   ]

Is the time of year important?   Yes [   ]   No [   ]

What is the lead time between the advertisement appearing and the customer reacting?

(a) To enquiry level?   [   ]   (days/weeks/months)

(b) To ordering?   [   ]   (days/weeks/months)

The examples below show the importance of accurately determining the advertising lead time to help optimise sales.

The sales pattern, which is similar to many durable household product sales patterns, is driven by the advertising. This campaign takes time to reach the bulk of its target market, and they in turn take time to consider the proposition before deciding to purchase. However once the sales build-up has started the response lag means that the advertising expenditure can be reduced even though sales continue to rise.

Advertising expenditure as a percentage of sales appears to be very high in some months of the campaign, but overall the average of 9 per cent is as forecast during the planning stage (see Figure 11.1 and 11.2).

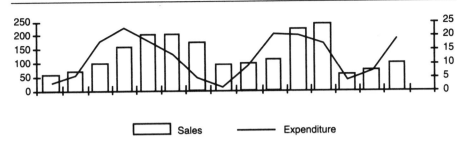

Sales   Expenditure

Figure 11.1   A typical advertising-led sales pattern (graph)

J	F	M	A	M	J	J	A	S	O	N	D	J	F	M

Advertising Expenditure £'000's

| 3 | 6 | 18 | 23 | 18 | 13 | 5 | 1 | 9 | 21 | 20 | 17 | 4 | 7 |

Sales £'000's

| 60 | 70 | 100 | 160 | 210 | 205 | 170 | 95 | 99 | 114 | 225 | 245 | 65 | 80 |

Total Sales £'000's   2003   Total Ad Spend £'000's   184

Figure 11.2   A typical advertising-led sales pattern (chart)

■ **Select the Appropriate Business Segments or Consumer Groups from Your Predetermined Target Audience**

Can you improve cost effectiveness by subdividing your target groups? Into how many segments can you subdivide the target groups you have already listed (Figure 11.3)?

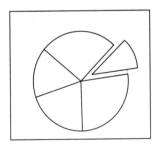

Figure 11.3   Target group segments

```
.....................................................................
.....................................................................
.....................................................................
```

■ **Select the Medium or Media that Your Target Segments are Most Likely to Respond to, or the Business or Lifestyle Lists that are Most Likely to Match Your Target's Characteristics**

- Is the position of the advertisement important?

- What size should it be?

- If you are using direct mail, will you get a better response by mailing to the home or the work address?

What media will you use to reach your target audience?

Media selection	Format or size
....	....
....	....
....	....

■ **Prepare the Media Plan**

This will provide a schedule of advertisements, editorial releases or mailing dates and sizes. The plan should include:

- Objectives: state the campaign objectives.

- Timescales: the campaign period.

- Budgets: the total cost of the campaign, including artwork, and also the expected sales or increases in sales.

- Frequency: this is the number of times a particular advertisement or message is scheduled to appear.

- Opportunities: this is an estimate of the number of times your target audience will see your advertisement.

- Reach: this is the overall percentage of your target audience that you expect will see your advertisement at least once.

What else do you need in your plan?

It is important to know what media apportunities are available to you, so you should prepare a media list. If you are marketing to the public in a limited geographical area you will need to know about local newspapers and commercial radio and television stations. If you are marketing to a specific industry you will to know about the publications produced for that particular trade.

For local newspapers you should list the necessary data in a table such as the one below, (most of you have computers so you can start a database table for rates):

Title	Phone no.	1 col. (£)	2 col. (£)	5 col. (£)	8 col. (£)	Linage per column

and a second table for other rate card information and special prices.

Title	Run of paper	Front page	Classified	Discounts & premiums

With this information you should put together your planned advertising schedule showing your weeky (or daily) budget by media. You can soon develop a spreadsheet or data model to help you model your activity. From your base information you can plan your media coverage by area, region and country (if appropriate) by week and month.

Area	Medium	Size	Cost	Weekly budget	Period total

Once the plan is developed you can monitor your weekly budget outlay to make sure it is remains within your total plan.

■ Consider Your Product or Service Features and Their Perceived Benefit to Your Consumer

List any unique attributes of your product (USP – Unique selling proposition). List any other benefits, and if applicable list them in the order of importance that would appeal to the different segments of your target market.

Note: whilst a feature may be important to you, it will only be important to your customers if they can obtain some benefit from it. A simple way to ensure that you have converted your feature to a customer benefit is to add 'this means that'. For example, our bread is baked on the premises, *this means that* it is always fresh.

List the USP's or product attributes and the benefits to the customer of each of your products.

Product attribute + 'this means that' =	Benefit

■ Prepare the Message

Determining the detail of the promotional messages should take place at this stage of the planning process so that both the headline and the body of the text can be orientated to appeal to the specific audience being addressed. The acronym AIDA is a useful memory tool to help you orientate your message to your target group:

- A – Attract Attention
- I – Raise Interest
- D – Create Desire
- A – Action, generate response, that is, 'call in today', 'phone for brochure now'

Don't forget segmentation; the same product aimed at different target segments of your market may require a variation of the message, especially the headlines, in order to hold the reader's attention. Figure 11.4 provides an indication of how to use AIDA when preparing your advertising message.

A I D A – Attract, Interest, Desire, Action

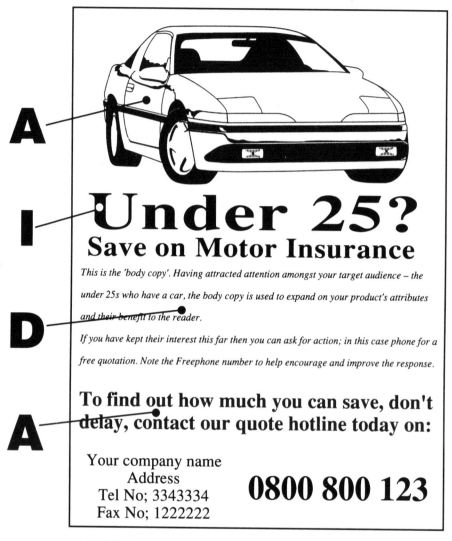

(**A I D A** – Attract, Interest, Desire, Action)

Figure 11.4   The fundamental components of an advertisement

■ Set Your Campaign in Motion

Monitor the responses as the plan develops, make adjustments as necessary and evaluate the final result against the campaign objectives determined at the beginning of the planning process.

- Measure
- Monitor
- Evaluate
- *And improve next time*

Remember, although choosing the right medium is most important, getting the message right as well can increase the overall response by as much as 100 per cent!

How will you monitor your campaign?

....
....
....
....

■   Summary of The Ten Point Plan for Advertising Success

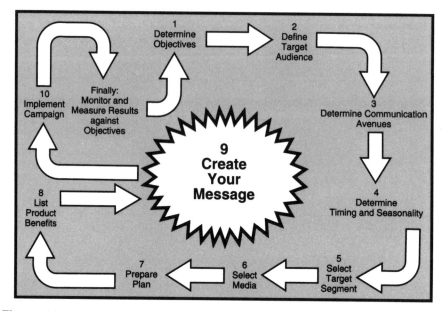

Figure 11.5   The ten point plan for advertising success

CHAPTER 12

Sales Promotions

Promotions are the lifeblood of all sales operations; they are the way to introduce products and services to potential customers and create extra volume sales.

Promotional activity is often called 'below the line' – traditionally this is because of where costs are shown on the profit and loss account (see Chapter 13), but now it is often called below the line because you cannot see it in the way that you can see advertising.

Before devising suitable promotions for your business it is important to be aware of the different types of promotion that can be used, including the following.

- **Competition/prize draw**   These can be fun but check that the type you use is not contrary to the law. If you have a competition you must include a test of skill – you cannot enter all purchasers in a draw because that constitutes a lottery.

- **Linked**   Purchase of item A allows a discount on item B. If you sell wine and someone else sells food it can work well to allow discount of a related item.

- **Money-off**   A simple system but it reduces profitability – see discussion below.

- **Multi-buy**   Two for the price of one. Three for the price of two.

- **Self-liquidators**   These are goods that qualifying customers can purchase at reduced rates to them, but at no cost to you.

- **Value added**   Extra goods obtained by the qualifying customers, such as vouchers towards the purchase of other goods (similar to self-liquidators); also extra volume at no extra price, as for most beer and lager brands these days.

- **Coupons**   Similar to money-off but through a qualifying coupon. Often a high proportion are not redeemed, but for planning purposes do not count on this.

- **Samples/trials**   Giving potential customers a chance to try the product or service.

- **Free gifts**   Obtained by mailing in tokens, labels and so on, or attached to the object being purchased (a drinking glass on a bottle and so on).

- **Events**   Event sponsorship, clinics and lectures, exhibition attendance.

- **Loyalty schemes**   Many leading retailers now focus on loyalty (see discussion on customer retention in Chapter 13).

  - Purchases through certain retailers or the use of certain credit cards earn air miles.

  - At least one petrol retailing chain has a loyalty bonus scheme helping customers earn points through the use of a smart card.

  - Some leading grocery retailers have club cards through which discounts are made on future purchases.

■ Which Promotion Should I Use?

■ Competitions and Prize Draws

These can be used to create excitement and interest. Also a small budget can be used quite effectively in the form of one substantial prize, for example a holiday. Be careful of draws as everybody must be allowed to enter with or without a purchase being made. Writing a slogan makes it a contest of skill and allows it to be limited to purchasers.

■ Linked

Linked promotions are very complicated and are generally best left to multiple retailers to administer through their complex computer systems.

■ Money-Off

A good way to stimulate sales – but remember it comes straight off the profits. In addition, if you are always reducing prices no one will buy the goods at the full price. Perhaps you do want to occupy this aggressive pricing position in the market, but be careful you do not become like a clothes fashion boutique that reduces prices by 50 per cent – no one buys till it has a sale. Or perhaps you *are* a fashion boutique.

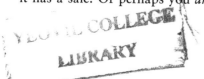

■ **Multi-Buy**

Often better than straight money-off, as at least you get increased volume in return for the discount.

■ **Self-Liquidators/Value Added**

Both these approaches achieve the same objective – the customer gets more because he/she buys from you, and the cost to you is zero or very low.

Self-liquidators or offers rely on your being able to buy goods at reduced prices and passing on the items at little or no margin. Value added items are things such as hotel vouchers. You can purchase these for little or no cost and you have an offer that has quite a high perceived value to your customer. In turn hoteliers are happy to accept these guests as they occupy rooms at quiet times of the year and are obliged to buy meals at the hotel, which pays for the cost of their stay.

It is very important to choose promotions that are consistent with your product and company position or image. If your goods are luxuries your promotions should not be cut-price. If your goods or services are value for money, then money off will be most effective.

■ Suitable Promotions for Business to Business

■ **Gifts**

Nearly all businesses have offices, so items with your name on act as constant reminders. Planners, diaries and notepads work well – one of the best has been a simple plastic holder for 3M's post-it notes.

■ **Incentives**

To develop business, 'recommend a friend' can be very effective. If orders are significant from the recommendations, a bottle of champagne is a small price to pay.

■ **Events**

If you want to make a mark then a reception party or event sponsorship may be appropriate – but do not get drawn into something that may look glamorous but does not enable you to reach the appropriate target customers.

For one of our clients, a funeral director, we organised a string quartet concert and invited specifiers, that is, doctors, coroner's staff and so on. There was no overt selling message, but an appropriately dignified promotion of the business was achieved.

■ Exhibitions

Exhibitions are clearly one of the best ways of meeting potential clients, most of whom will head for specific exhibits to find out about new products. It is important to thoroughly evaluate the time costs involved in taking part in the exhibition and soberly work out whether there is a potential return.

For example a client of ours – a primary food grower – took part in consumer attended exhibitions, where he introduced the public to his product. We calculated that his time and money was much better spent getting to know the wholesale trade and motivating them to educate retailers, who would in turn introduce his product to the general public. Far more customers would be reached more quickly by following this route.

■ Lectures and Seminars

Holding lectures and seminars establishes you as an authority on your subject. Your peers may then refer to you for specialist action. This is a particularly useful promotional method for professional practices.

■ Clinics

Inviting potential clients to venues where you can provide free consultation or advice sessions creates goodwill and often leads to invitations to tender.

■ Linked Promotions

Manufacturers and suppliers should leave linked promotions to multiple retailers who have the computerised systems to deal with them. However if you are a retailer you can devise your own limited promotions to help move stock. Some examples are reasonably obvious, such as:

- Sports shop's offering reduced-priced tennis balls or clothing with a new racquet.
- Cycle shop offering helmets and so on at lower prices with new bicycles.

There are clearly good opportunities for linked promotions when the buyer of item A has good cause to buy item B. A reasonable incentive will probably push the buyer over the decision precipice!

CHAPTER 13

Marketing Service: Customer Care

In earlier chapters we discussed how good marketing involves knowing your customers and treating them appropriately to ensure the maximum return on your effort

■ The Importance of Customer Care

Why is customer care important? Certainly we all prefer someone to smile at us and say 'Have a nice day', even if they do not mean it, but evidence exists that companies who produce a service that their customers consider to be superior to that of their competitors achieve significantly better results, including:

- Higher selling prices.
- Better sales growth.
- Higher market share.

Whilst many businesses believe they are entirely customer focused, many of them still focus on selling their products and services rather than on determining supply and what customers want. They forget that it is not the product that makes the profit, it is the customers.

It is worth reminding ourselves of the 'What market are you in?' exercise in an earlier chapter.

If the business attends to A rather than B it will surely suffer as it will not provide what the customer wants.

Customer care can help us to focus on the real purpose of business, as expressed in the definition of marketing, namely satisfying customer needs profitably.

Concern	(A) What it thinks it does	(B) What it actually does
A bus company	Runs a bus service	Provides transportation
A baker	Bakes and sells bread	Provides food
A cinema	Shows films	Provides a source of entertainment
Your business		

■ The Principles of Customer Care

Over the years various principles for customer care have been established. As long as you understand the basic principles you can develop a customer care policy for your business.

It has been estimated that the cost of recruiting a new customer is as much as thirteen times higher than the cost of retaining an existing one. Obviously it is much more cost effective to encourage established customers to repurchase than to have continually to seek new ones.

The concept of the lifetime value of a customer is well established. Many companies now calculate what a customer is worth to them in terms of total potential sales revenue. For car manufacturers this can be a very substantial amount and even for businesses such as pizza delivery companies the long-term sales value can run well into four figures.

Equally well established is the bad news syndrome – an unhappy customer may not tell the supplier but will tell many potential users. Various estimates of this include:

- Travellers that have had poor flights tell seventeen others.

- An unhappy pub user tells thirteen others.

- A dental practice running on the 3–11 rule: if you look after someone, he or she will tell three others, if you do not look after them eleven others will get to know.

The opposite of dissatisfied customers telling many of their misfortune is recommendation and positive word of mouth – often the most powerful method of recruiting new customers.

Other important points to note are that:

- Regular customers buy more and are serviced more efficiently.

- Retaining customers makes it more difficult for competitors to increase their market share.

- The prices you are able to charge is the result of the perceived level of customer care that you provide.

■ The Need for Customer Retention

Modern trading methods increase the need for customer retention through customer care as the advance of technology has resulted in the arrival of many competing products that appear very similar, making their market just a commodity market. If the products are indistinguishable, then naturally customers will tend to choose the best supplier.

■ Customer Service Standards

■ Is the Customer Satisfied?

Although most businesses have introduced a customer care policy, in many of these businesses attitudes towards customers and actual standards of customer service have changed very little during the last five years. Customers are likely to become confused, dissatisfied or angry when the services they receive appears to differ widely from the standard they anticipate. This dissatisfaction is heightened when a monopoly is the culprit and there is no choice or no alternative supplier is available. When there is plenty of choice the customers take their business elsewhere.

The question that anyone responsible for customer service should continually ask themselves is *'Do I know if ALL our employees are providing ALL our customers with the correct level of service all the time?'*

The effectiveness of a customer care policy that does not include some method of monitoring and evaluating customer attitudes cannot be measured accurately and differing attitudes and deviations from agreed standards are almost certain to appear. The difference between a business or organisation's declared customer-care service statement and the level of service that a significant proportion of its customers actually receive can usually be ascribed to one or more of the following:

- Weak management.
- Lack of, or insufficient staff training.

■ Weak Management

A weak management structure in any organisation is often caused by a combination of individual managers being insufficiently trained at operational level, unclear objectives and indecisive leadership. These factors will tend to negate any attempt to introduce policy changes issued solely as policy documents or internal memoranda, and will also hamper the development of any kind of team spirit other than an inward-looking protectionist one.

> If the employees in an organisation don't have a sense of purpose or feel that it doesn't matter what they think or say because nothing will change, what chance has a customer care policy of succeeding, especially if the employees feel it has been imposed by senior managers, or see it as indecisive, or it arrives as a dictate from a remote head office.
>
> *It is no good telling your customers that you care about them if you don't show your staff how to care and keep caring.*

■ Lack of, or Insufficient, Staff Training

One of the mistakes most commonly made among apparently caring businesses appears to be that having invested the time and money needed to develop and implement a customer care policy and train staff, the constant need to react to day-to-day pressures takes over from the planned approach. As a result the business managers revert to their old ways and the continued training of existing employees and even the initial training of new employees is simply forgotten or given a low priority.

Think about any differences you can identify between declared policies and actual customer care attitudes within the businesses or organisations you have worked for or that you deal with, and then complete the following exercise.

Organisation/business	Do they have a customer care policy?	Is the actual or perceived level of service better or worse?
1. An NHS trust	. . . .	
2. A large telecommunications company	. . . .	
3. Your district/city county council	. . . .	
4. Your local garage	. . . .	
5. A multiple retailer	. . . .	
6. A government department	. . . .	
7. A trade organisation (chamber of commerce, TEC, business link or enterprise agency)	. . . .	
8. The business you work for now	. . . .	

How does your business compare with others you know?

. . . .

. . . .

What conclusions can you draw from the above?

. . . .

. . . .

■ Cost-Benefit of Customer Service

Different customers will buy different amounts from you and they will cost different amounts to service. Analysis of your customer base will generally indicate that some of your customers are much more profitable than others. Many businesses often eliminate the 'tail' of their customer base on the ground that they are expensive to service.

Certainly analysis of all the activities involved in servicing an account will often indicate that certain customers yield no net profit at all. It is quite important that such analyses are performed – once you have done the analysis you can decide what to do about the various types of customer you have.

You may decide to lower your service standards, although all recent experiences and the philosophy of successful service companies suggest that this is an unsound practice. Alternatively you may try to increase the price paid by that customer, for example by offering lower and lower discounts. On the other hand you may decide that the customer in question has the potential to become better and more profitable for you and that you will continue with your present level of service.

In your account-servicing analysis you will need to include the cost and relative effect of the following:

- Pricing and discounting

- Account management

- Order processing costs

- Promotional costs

- Customer-specific packaging and inventory costs

- Transport

- Credit

■ Customer Service Standards of Some Firms

Leading firms these days put heavy emphasis on customer care along the following lines.

- Exceeding customers' expectations.

- Every complaint dealt with quickly.

- Exceptional service is the only service.

- 100 per cent satisfaction 100 per cent of the time.

■ Customer Service Levels

Now that you can see it pays to have a good standard of customer care you should consider the elements of customer care and ascertain your present level of competence.

In the table provided (Figure 13.1) indicate which elements are relevant to you according to the scale of 1–7 at the top of the table. In the 'Your rating' column, enter your assessment of your present business performance based on the scale of 1–10 below.

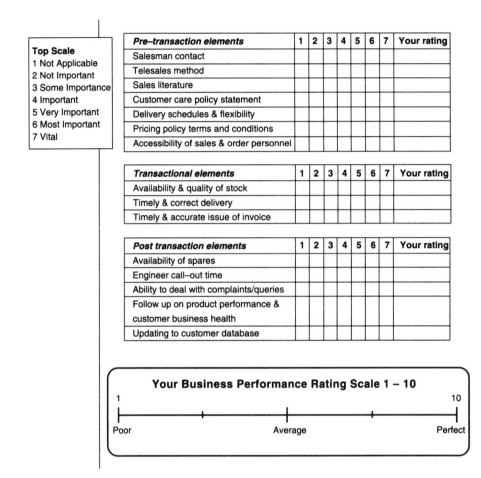

Top Scale
1 Not Applicable
2 Not Important
3 Some Importance
4 Important
5 Very Important
6 Most Important
7 Vital

Pre–transaction elements	1	2	3	4	5	6	7	Your rating
Salesman contact								
Telesales method								
Sales literature								
Customer care policy statement								
Delivery schedules & flexibility								
Pricing policy terms and conditions								
Accessibility of sales & order personnel								

Transactional elements	1	2	3	4	5	6	7	Your rating
Availability & quality of stock								
Timely & correct delivery								
Timely & accurate issue of invoice								

Post transaction elements	1	2	3	4	5	6	7	Your rating
Availability of spares								
Engineer call–out time								
Ability to deal with complaints/queries								
Follow up on product performance & customer business health								
Updating to customer database								

Your Business Performance Rating Scale 1 – 10

1   10

Poor   Average   Perfect

Figure 13.1 Customer service levels chart

■ Customer Care Strengths and Weaknesses

Following on from your last analysis, you should note which elements of customer care are strengths and consider how you might exploit them, and which are your customer care weaknesses and consider what action you should take to remedy them.

Customer care strengths	How can we improve?
Customer care weaknesses	**What actions will minimise the weakness?**

■ Developing Your Customer Care Package

Before you can develop a customer care package you need to consider the various elements it should contain. Your customer care package will be influenced by your mission statement and the objectives you have established. Examples of mission statements might be:

- To be the best product provider in the region.
- To provide the best value-for-money service in the region.

Your customer care policy will be determined by which of the above you intend to be. If you are going to be the *best* you will have to provide a high level of care and service. If you are going to provide the *best value for money* then customers will expect you to be efficient and economical in order to secure the price advantages you are offering.

Once you have decided on your service elements and levels they should be recorded in a procedures service manual. All your staff should see this and understand it. They need to know how to apply it and if necessary training should be given. In addition a statement of service policy and standards should be made available to your customers. Knowing what service levels you are aiming for can be reassuring to your customers and can also be used as a positive selling tool.

■ Service Level Strategy

Having decided on your service elements you need to determine the level of service you are going to provide. Certain customers and products will be on a nearly 100 per cent service level whereas others will not be supported to quite the same extent.

Customer name/type	Service level (%)

■ Allocation of Resources

You need to make conscious decisions about the allocation of resources. This will apply particularly to:

● Frequency of representative visits.

● Level of stock held.

● Speed of response to telephone and postal enquiries.

● Speed of response by service engineers.

You should calculate the cost of the service level you plan to implement for each customer.

■ Monitor and Control Procedures

Having introduced customer care you will require procedures to make sure the system is working.

■ Customer Feedback

This can take several forms, including customer questionnaires, either self-completion or by telephone contact.

■ Mystery Shopper

Mystery shopping as a way of testing service procedures is a high-growth industry. It can work very well for hotels, restaurants, banks, garages and most retail trades via personal visits by the mystery shopper or through telephone contact. Your receptionist is the first contact and sets the tone and atmosphere as far as the customer is concerned.

■ Complaints Procedures

As part of your customer care package you should have established a procedure for dealing with complaints, as well as a system for recording the level of complaints. Part of your plan should be to set an acceptable complaint level (perhaps zero?) and investigate what is going wrong with the business when complaints rise above this level.

How does your business measure its customer care performance?

```
....................................................................................................
....................................................................................................
....................................................................................................
```

■ Quality Assurance

Having established a service level you need a system to ensure that this level is maintained. Consistency can be achieved by introducing quality monitoring and systems such as ISO 9000, although for a small company the implementation costs can be expensive. You can also achieve consistency by making sure your service and quality procedures are well documented and that someone in the firm is responsible for monitoring the standards achieved.

It is important that the management are dedicated to achieving the agreed level of customer care, otherwise the rest of the team will only pay lip service to the policy.

It seems that nowadays successful organisations have high levels of customer care. This must be your aim.

CHAPTER 14

Planning: Putting the Numbers Together

In the preceding chapters we have discussed most of the components of the planning process initially illustrated in Chapter 1. In this chapter we will look at the numeric elements of the planning process and explain the principles behind those numbers.

In Part 2 you will find various planning forms where you can enter your figures.

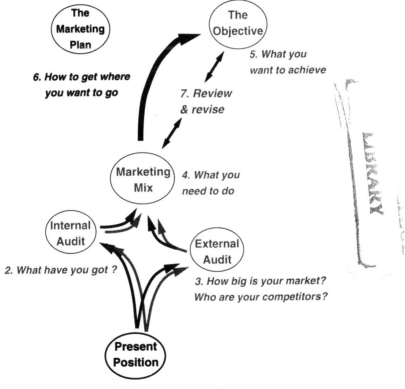

Figure 14.1 The marketing planning process

■ Developing the Profit and Loss Account

Assuming you have an opening balance sheet or a statement of assets and liabilities (such as debtors and creditors), the numeric part of planning results in a forecast profit and loss account – from this you can produce a cash flow forecast and closing balance sheet or asset movement sheet for the period in question.

The elements of the numeric plan may vary, but in principle the plan can be developed as follows.

First, calculate the market size in convenient units (as discussed before) the size of the market in which you will operate and your forecast as to how it will develop over the planning period (steady, grow, decline and, if measured in currency units, the effect of inflation).

Second, estimate your share – will it stay steady or increase over the period? You may be concerned with several markets, sectors or products and each may perform differently, and as a consequence you will need to create separate forecasts of markets, sectors and shares.

Third, if you can forecast sales by sectors or sales channels that have distinctly different prices then you should do so. It is best at this stage to be as detailed as possible. Sales should be in units at this point, for example cars sold, professional hours or days sold and so on. This should be converted to revenue sales by extending at your average selling price. Do not include VAT in your profit and loss account forecast, – although it will certainly be significant in your cash flow forecast.

Fourth, your sales forecasts by product or by market sector can be calculated by multiplying your share of the appropriate market by the market size. Now you have an annual forecast of your sales you can produce a monthly forecast.

Fifth, the next calculation is cost of sales. This includes all costs that arise in the purchase or manufacture of goods and their sale. If you are buying products the cost of sales is likely to include the purchase price minus discounts and any carriage or transport costs. If you are making the products you are selling, costs to be included may include all material costs, labour costs, transportation, storage and machinery depreciation. It is possible to have a heated debate on what can or should be included in costs of sales. At the end of the day true costs should be included in such a way that you can see that selling or producing the product or service can be seen to be *genuinely* contributing to income over and above what the business was earning before the product was introduced.

Individual cost of sale calculations need to be undertaken for every product or product range, but for sales planning and profit and loss account planning purposes only the total unit cost need be used in the forecast.

Sixth, after subtracting cost of sales from net sales (that is sales less discounts), you have the gross profit or margin.

Seventh, the next items are the sales costs – salespersons' salaries, commission, expenses, marketing costs (advertising, promotions and publicity when associated with products and services) and departmental costs.

Eighth, the net revenue after all these deductions will be the contribution to other overheads. These will invariably be the fixed costs of operating the business: the building, the establishment, administration, staff, and legal and professional costs.

Finally, what is left is your net profit before interest, tax and dividends.

In summary, the profit and loss account forecast is created as follows:

1. Market size forecast.
2. Share forecast.
3. Unit sales (market size × share).
4. Revenue = sales × (unit selling price – net discounts).
5. Cost of sales = sales × (unit costs).
6. Gross margin = revenue – cost of sales.
7. Sales and marketing costs are calculated.
8. Contribution to overhead = Gross margin – sales and marketing costs.
9. Net margin before interest and tax = contribution – overheads.

If you find that the result of the above calculation is zero or close to zero, do not just forecast sales upward to cover the deficit. You have a problem – how can you reduce your overheads or cut other costs? Can you put prices up – are you charging too little? (this is possible, although unlikely.)

■ The Cash Flow

The monthly cash flow is calculated from the monthly profit and loss account. For profit and loss purposes a sale occurs when an invoice is issued but normally only a cash retailer will get the money at once. For most businesses a certain proportion of invoices are paid in 30 days or less, with other proportions being paid in 60, 90 or even 120 days. Once you know what percentage of your sales invoices are paid each month, you can construct your revenue forecast by transferring each month's sales from your profit and loss forecast into the relevant month in the cash flow forecast.

Cost of sales, sales costs and other overheads can be treated in exactly the same way. Sales costs that appear in your profit and loss forecast are not necessarily paid at the end of every month, so these can be apportioned appropriately.

You will need to forecast your revenue flow by performing a calculation to include VAT (unless you wish to run a separate VAT control). Similarly with your costs and expenses, invoices will arise when goods are ordered or delivered, but you may be paying *pro forma* or at 30-, 60- or 90-day intervals. Other items such as wages are normally paid monthly.

You can see from the above the way a net cash flow forecast can be developed from the forecast profit and loss account. Amounts outstanding at the end of the period, debtors, trade creditors, bank funds and so on. are all items that will affect your forecast balance sheet in one way or another.

■ The Forecast Balance Sheet

The balance sheet forecast shows how your net worth has changed by the end of the forecast period. It shows the difference between assets and liabilities.

Assets are:

- Buildings
- Stock
- Debtors
- Investments

Liabilities are:

- Creditors
- Overdrafts
- Loans

If your asset to liability ratio decreases (or becomes negative) in your forecast period, then you have a problem. Have *another* look at your forecasts!

PART II
The Marketing Planner:
Marketing Planning Forms

CHAPTER 15

The Marketing Planner

The forms in this planner have been prepared by consultants who between them have accumulated almost fifty years of experience of providing advice to businesses and organisations of all types and who have prepared literally thousands of marketing strategies, business plans and other reports for businesses of all sizes.

The primary objective is to make your business life easier by providing you with a fast and simple, easy to use marketing planning system.

The forms in the following sections have been designed to guide you through the complete marketing planning process. The sections are:

(A) Primary Information

(B) The Operating Environment

(C) Marketing and Sales Operating Parameters

(D) Global Overheads and Contributions

(E) Profit and Loss Forecasting

(F) Cash Flow Forecasting

Using this planner in conjunction with the text in Part 1 will not only help you fully understand the marketing concept, but will enable you to prepare comprehensive marketing plans, including sales and financial forecasts.

As well as marketing strategy preparation, the forms allow realistic planning of almost any marketing scenario and virtually any type of business, including:

● Marketing communications, budget planning.

● New product launch planning.

● New business start-up.

● Sales management control and sales forecast.

● Cash flows and other financial forecasts for bankers and other lending institutions.

To help speed up your plan preparation we suggest you first gather together as much relevant background information and financial data as possible. This information could include the previous two years' audited or management accounts, sales and purchase ledger entries, and selling costs and marketing expenditure for prior years.

■ (A) Primary Information

■ Title Page

A
Marketing Strategy
for

....

....

for the period

From: ..../.........../.........

To: ..../.........../.........

Prepared by

....

Date: ....

This is an example of a title page for your report. Photocopy it and type in the appropriate information.

■ **Form A1: Background Information**

This form gathers together the basic information that is needed for the introductory page of your report.

| A1 | Background Information

1. Your business or organisation's name:

2. Trading division or departmental name if different from above:

3. What type of business or organisation is it?

4. Plan title

5. Forecast period   months/years

    from   to

    (month and year only)   (month and year only)

6. Who is the author of this plan?

7. Who is the plan being prepared for?

8. Date prepared

■ **Form A2: The Internal Audit – Business and Financial Structure**

Every plan needs background information and this form helps you draw together and structure the financial background of your business. Whilst you may not feel that some of the financial summaries are relevant, say, if you are a divisional marketing manager of a large company, the information could be very important to your plan if you are running a small business that needs additional funds and you want to prepare a report for your bank manager.

A2   The Internal Audit – Business and Financial Structure

1.   Year established [　　　　　]   2. Business format [　　　　　]

3.   End of financial year
     or other accounting period [　　　　　]

4.   Major shareholders, partners or other key owners   % share

   (a) [　　　　　　　　　]   [　　　　　]

   (b) [　　　　　　　　　]   [　　　　　]

   (c) [　　　　　　　　　]   [　　　　　]

   (d) [　　　　　　　　　]   [　　　　　]

   (e) | all others [　　　　　]   [　　　　　]

                                    100%

5.   At the end of the last financial year or accounting period, retaining funds were:

   £ [　　　　　]

6.   At the end of the last accounting period, loans or HP outstanding amounted to:

Type	Balance outstanding	Monthly payment	Months to complete	Final payment
(a) [　　　　　]	£ [　　]	£ [　　]	[　　]	[　　]
(b) [　　　　　]	£ [　　]	£ [　　]	[　　]	[　　]
(c) (all others)	£ [　　]	£ [　　]	[　　]	[　　]

7.   Total overdraft facilities and amounts outstanding at the end of the last accounting period:

Lender	Limit	Outstanding
(a) [　　　　　　　]	£ [　　]	£ [　　]
(b) [　　　　　　　]	£ [　　]	£ [　　]
(c) [　　　　　　　]	£ [　　]	£ [　　]

8.   The business has cash in hand, on deposit or other realisable assets amounting to:

Item	Amount	Approximate withdrawal time
(a) [　　　　　　　]	£ [　　]	£ [　　]
(b) [　　　　　　　]	£ [　　]	£ [　　]
(c) [　　　　　　　]	£ [　　]	£ [　　]

■   **Form A3: The Internal Audit – Product or Product Group Sales by Region**

This form gathers together basic information regarding your products and where they are sold. Enter the product or service name in the appropriate box. If you sell more than six products or services enter the main product groups or service groups on this page.

If you need more room for products or product groups just photocopy the additional sheets required, don't forget to bring forward the percentage subtotals to your master form.

Enter in the regional percentage boxes your estimates of the percentage of sales for each product or service (or product and service group) derived from each region.

A3 The Internal Audit – Product/Product Group Sales by Region

Product sales by geographic region

Product/product group	Local area (%)	Regional (%)	All UK (%)	Europe (%)	Other (%)	Total (100%)
A						
B						
C						
D						
E						
F						

Comments:
. . . .
. . . .
. . . .

■ **Form A4: The Internal Audit – Distribution Channels and Distribution Margins by Major Product or Product Group**

This form will help you to organise your distribution channels into customer type and to consider the operating mark-up that each level of the distribution chain expects.

1. To maintain continuity enter the product or service names in the same order as the previous form.

2. Enter the product/service unit or average sales value, margin and distribution channel.

3. Enter the customer type in the 'first level' box, that is, importer, wholesaler, type of retailer (for many products/services – for example those sold direct to the public or to major multiples – there is often only one distribution level).

4. Enter the percentage mark-up to be added to the unit cost and calculate the value.

5. If further distribution levels are required, enter the percentage mark-up required – the new sell-on price should be calculated according to the previous sell-on price.

6. The final sell-on price or the manufacturer's suggested price (this used to be known as the recommended retail price or RRP, or the net book value for books and magazines) is calculated in the last box of each column.

7. Two total percentages can be calculated: (a) total margin and (b) total sell-on cost percentage.

   (a) Total percentage margin: this is calculated from the sales value back to the unit price.

   (b) Total sell-on cost percentage: this is the total percentage increase, or mark-up, from the unit price to the final sell-on price.

Total selling cost percentage: This is the total percentage increase, or mark-up, from the unit price to the final sell-on price.

A4 The Internal Audit – Distribution Channels and Distribution Margins by Major Product or Product Group

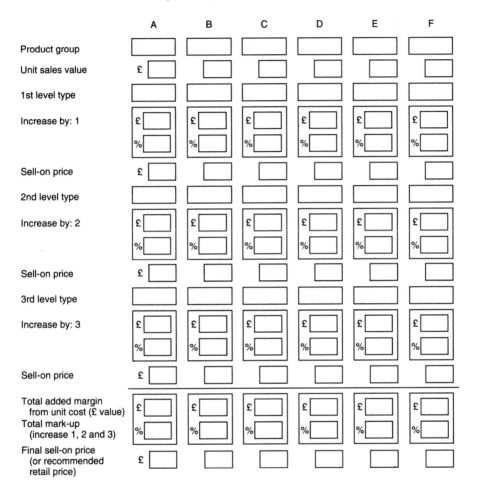

■ (B) The Operating Environment

Section B deals with some of the basic macro-environmental factors that could affect the outcome of your plan. Macro-environmental factors are those outside your direct control but which have a direct influence on your business. This section is divided into three main areas:

● The economic factors that could affect your plan.

● Customer profiles.

● The size of the market and your position in it (market share).

For further information see Chapter 3 in Part I.

■ Form B1: The External Audit – The Macro Environment

Completing form B1 will provide you with data to act as a guide when you are preparing your forecasts. But these figures will become out of date as time passes, so as with all forecasts they should be replaced with actual data and revised future trends.

B1 The External Audit – The Macro Environment

1. What is the current bank borrowing rate? [ ] %

2. What do you expect the average level of bank base rates to be in:

[ ] [ ] [ ] [ ] [ ] [ ] [ ]

6 months 12 months 18 months 24 months 3 years 4 years 5 years

3. What is the average current business bank deposit rate? [ ] %

4. What do you expect the average level of deposit rates to be in:

[ ] [ ] [ ] [ ] [ ] [ ] [ ]

6 months 12 months 18 months 24 months 3 years 4 years 5 years

5. What is the current annual rate of inflation? [ ] %

6. By what % rate do you expect inflation to increase or decrease during the following periods?

[ ] [ ] [ ] [ ] [ ] [ ] [ ]

6 months 1 year 18 months 2 years 3 years 4 years 5 years

7. Is your business affected by changing employment trends?

If yes, tick the appropriate boxes   Age group   Male   Female

National [ ]   16–24   [ ] [ ]

Regional [ ]   25–44   [ ] [ ]

Local [ ]   45–60   [ ] [ ]

8. Is your business sensitive to changing population trends? If yes tick the appropriate boxes.

National [ ]   0–15   [ ] [ ]

Regional [ ]   16–44   [ ] [ ]

Local [ ]   45–64   [ ] [ ]

                    65+   [ ] [ ]

Comments

[....]

■ Form B2: The External Audit – Customer Types

Enter the product group or product names in the same order as previously.

1. *Sales by product type.*   Enter the value of sales for the last year for each product or product group and calculate the percentage this represents of total sales. You can clearly illustrate the value of each product's sales by entering the percentages on the pie chart below the table.

2. *Sales by customer type.*   List your main customers, or customer types in the boxes marked 1–6 at the bottom of the page. For product A decide which of the customer types you have listed are the most important buyers of that product and what percentage of total sales they represent. Enter the customer number in the first open box in the 'sales by customer type' section and the percentage of product A's sales for which they account. Consider the next most important customer group, then enter their number and the percentage of total sales they account for in the next box. Complete the rest of the boxes using 'others' at the end of each row to act as a balancing factor to ensure the total of each row always adds up to 100 per cent.

   If you want to produce a chart of your sales by customer type, mark off the percentages for each customer type by product on the appropriate horizontal bar of the chart. Each bar equals 100 per cent and each section marked is equal to 25 per cent. Insert the customer type or customer number in the relevant section. Examples of customer types will vary depending on the products. Some common examples could be:

   ● Business products: hotel and catering, construction, professional services.

   ● Construction: local authority, manufacturing, main contractors, commercial.

   ● Consumer: male, female, married, single, car owners, boat owners.

B2 The External Audit – Product Sales by Customer Type

The main products sold are:

% Sales by customer type

Product/product group type	Value last year	% of total sales	% No.	% No.	% No.	Others % No.		Total
A	£	%					=	100%
B	£	%					=	100%
C	£	%					=	100%
D	£	%					=	100%
E	£	%					=	100%
F	£	%					=	100%
Total sales	£	100 %					=	100%

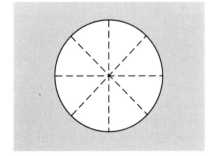

% Sales by product type

(Each segment of the pie chart is equal to a 12.5% share)

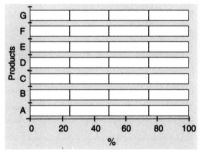

% Sales by customer type

(Each segment of the bar chart is equal to a 25% share)

Our main customer types are:

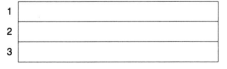

1
2
3

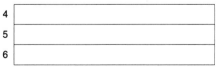

4
5
6

■ **Form B3: The External Audit – Market Size**

List your product groups as before and also the sales by product (from form B2).

If the products sell in different markets (or different segments of the market) estimate the market size for each. To calculate your product's percentage share of this market, divide 'our sales' by ' market size' and multiply the answer by 100.

Repeat this procedure for the other products. The remaining boxes should be filled in when you have completed form B3.1.

B3   The External Audit – Market Size

Figures based on the last financial year, which was 19

Product or product group	Sales last year (£)	Est. of market size	Our share (%)	Main competitor's market share				
				1 (%)	2 (%)	3 (%)	4 (%)	Others (%)
A								
B								
C								
D								
E								
F								
G								

■ Form B3.1: The Exernal Audit – Competitor Analysis (a)

Next list the main competitors for each of your products. You will probably be surprised how many different competitors you can identify, especially if you have a diverse product or service range and you sell in a number of different markets or market segments.

To extimate their market share, calculate each competitor's sales by product, divide this figure by the 'market size' then multiply by 100. Enter your competitor's numbers and the percentages obtained for them in the appropriate product row box on form B3. Ensure that the 'our share' box plus the other percentages in each row add up to 100.

B3.1 The External Audit – Competitor Analysis (a)

The main competitors for each of our products are:

Product or product groups

	A	B	C	D	E	F
1. Competitor name						
Sales last year	£	£	£	£	£	£
2. Competitor name						
Sales last year	£	£	£	£	£	£
3. Competitor name						
Sales last year	£	£	£	£	£	£
4. Competitor name						
Sales last year	£	£	£	£	£	£

■ Form B3.2: The External Audit – Competitor Analysis (b)

List your main competitors in the order that you consider them to present a threat to your business. Consider the position of each competitor in the Boston Matrix grid. The size of the circle provides an indication of relative size. Mark the position of each competitor on the matrix using the appropriate size circle and their number. For more information on how to use the Boston Matrix see Chapter 10, 'Forecasting'. When you have finished you should consider your position on the chart relative to those of your competitors.

An example could be as follows:

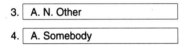

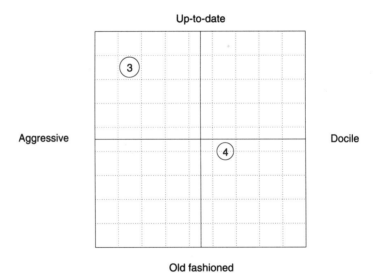

B3.2 | The External Audit – Competitor Analysis (b)

List your main competitors in order of 'threat':

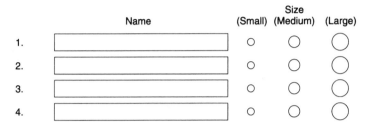

	Name	Size (Small)	(Medium)	(Large)
1.		○	○	○
2.		○	○	○
3.		○	○	○
4.		○	○	○

Mark relative competitor positions:

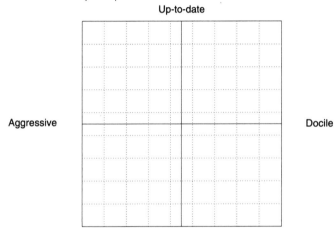

Comments

■ Forms B4.1 – B4.7: The Marketing Mix

The marketing mix provides you with a framework against which you can evaluate your products(s) or service(s).

The following section contains the seven P's. The first four are applicable to business and organisations selling products and product ranges. The last three 'P's are optional for these businesses and organisations, but essential for those that are primarily service related, those providing advisory services or those selling intangibles such as insurance. For a detailed explanation of the marketing mix see Chapter 5, 'Market Appraisal: The Marketing Mix'.

To complete this product mix, consider carefully how important each of the product attributes listed are to your business (is your view likely to be the same as that of your customers?)

Tick one of the boxes in columns 1–7 for each item on the list. The scale of importance is shown below the table and ranges from 1 (not applicable, meaning you don't have to consider the item as it is not part of your product's characteristics), to 7 (vital, meaning that your product or even your business will fail if this aspect is neglected). Note: only a proportion of relevant attributes should score 6 or 7.

B4.1 The Marketing Mix – The Product

Product Attributes

The importance of the various elements of the product mix are:	1	2	3	4	5	6	7
Quality							
Feature and options							
Style or styling							
The brand, product or service name							
Packaging							
Warranty							
Service support							
Range							
Cost (materials or buying-in price)							
Patent, trademark or copyright							
Sales office							
Order office							

Scale of importance:

1. Not applicable
2. Not important
3. Some importance
4. Important
5. Very important
6. Most important
7. Vital

B4.2 The Marketing Mix – The Price

Price Attributes

The importance of the various elements of the pricing mix are:	1	2	3	4	5	6	7
Pricing level							
Discount policy							
Credit terms							
Payment methods							

Scale of importance:

1. Not applicable
2. Not important
3. Some importance
4. Important
5. Very important
6. Most important
7. Vital

B4.3   The Marketing Mix – The Place

The Place

The importance of the various elements of the place or distribution mix are:	1	2	3	4	5	6	7
Distribution channels							
Distribution coverage							
Outlet location							
Sales territories							
Inventory levels and locations							
Transportation							
Product positioning							
Product perception							

Scale of importance:

1. Not applicable
2. Not important
3. Some importance

4. Important
5. Very important

6. Most important
7. Vital

B4.4   The Marketing Mix – The Promotion

The Promotion

The importance of the various elements of the promotion mix are:	1	2	3	4	5	6	7
Advertising							
Selling							
Promotion							
Publicity							

Scale of importance:

1. Not applicable
2. Not important
3. Some importance

4. Important
5. Very important

6. Most important
7. Vital

B4.5   The Marketing Mix – The People

The People

The importance to the marketing mix of the people who come into contact with the customer are:	1	2	3	4	5	6	7
Friendliness							
Presentability							
Helpfulness							
Approachability							
Politeness							
Knowledge							
Competence							

Scale of importance:

1. Not applicable   4. Important   6. Most important
2. Not important   5. Very important   7. Vital
3. Some importance

B4.6   The Marketing Mix – The Presence

The Presence

The importance to the marketing mix of the various elements of the business or organisation's physical presence or public face are:	1	2	3	4	5	6	7
Operational:							
Size							
Premises							
Corporate image							
Environment:							
Ambience							
Comfort							
Facilities							
Cleanliness							

Scale of importance:

1. Not applicable   4. Important   6. Most important
2. Not important   5. Very important   7. Vital
3. Some importance

B4.7   The Marketing Mix – The Process

The Process

The importance to the marketing mix of the various elements of the business process are:	1	2	3	4	5	6	7
Speed							
Efficiency							
Service time							
Waiting time							
Appointment system							
Forms and documents							

Scale of importance:

1. Not applicable   4. Important   6. Most important
2. Not important   5. Very important 7. Vital
3. Some importance

Repeat this analysis for each of the other elements of the marketing mix.

■ **Form B4.8: The Marketing Mix – The Key Ingredients**

The key ingredients of the marketing mix can now be summarised in order of importance on this form.

List all the items you have marked vital (number 7) on forms B4.1–4.7. Repeat this process listing all those marked most important (number 6) then, if you have any spaces left, those marked with a number 5 and so on.

If necessary continue on to a separate sheet. The completed list should be treated as an important checklist at the marketing planning stage.

When preparing your plan you should consider each item, reassess it and ask yourself the following questions:

1. Is this the appropriate level within your planning timescale?

   ● If not, then what is?

2. If it is the appropriate level:

   ● Is it being achieved?

   ● If not, what resources, effort and costs are required to achieve it?

| B4.8 | The Marketing Mix – Key Ingredients |

Rank No.	Item	Related 'P'	Importance value (7s and 6s only)
1			
2			
3			
4			
5			
6			
7			
8			
9			
10			
11			
12			
13			
14			
15			
16			
17			
18			
19			
20			

■ Forms B5.1–B5.4: SWOT Analysis

Forms B5.1 to B5.4 help you to summarise the information you have gathered so far into a SWOT (Strengths, Weaknesses, Opportunities and Threats) analysis.

Your SWOT analysis should be as objective as possible. It is a very important part of the planning process as without the assessment of the present state of your business and the market place that it can provide the plan that you prepare is less likely to succeed. For further information see Chapter 6 in Part II.

B5.1   SWOT Analysis – Strengths

The strengths of our business are:

These strengths can be developed further by:

B5.2   SWOT Analysis – Weaknesses

The weaknesses of our business or organisation within the market place are:

The steps required to correct these weaknesses are:

B5.3   SWOT Analysis – Opportunities

Opportunities that the business or organisation might be able to take advantage of are:

The resources and effort required and the benefit would be:

Resources and effort:

Benefit:

Resources and effort:

Benefit:

Resources and effort:

Benefit:

B5.4   SWOT Analysis – Threats

Factors within the business or organisation or from the external environment that could threaten the successful implementation of this plan are:

The steps that can be taken to minimise these threats and the costs involved are:

Steps:

Costs:

Steps:

Costs:

Steps:

Costs:

■ Form B6.1: The Mission Statement

The mission statement or charter statement is the written expression of your organisation's operating philosophy or ethos. It can be a simple statement encompassing all aspects of the operation or it can refer to individual factors such as:

- Customer/supplier relations.
- Buying policies.
- Attitudes towards employees.

Secondary mission statements (box 2) are often defined as 'charter' statements, for example suppliers' charter, patients' charter and so on.

Remember that your mission statement provides the overall framework of policies within which all objectives and operational procedures must be achievable – the mission statement is how you want to operate.

B6.1   The Mission Statement

Our mission statement is as follows:

Our secondary mission statement or individual charter statements are:

■ Form B6.2: The Strategic Business Objective

Setting strategic business objectives (within the framework of the mission statement) establishes targets for the future and provides a focus for all of the organisation's activities.

Set the five-year objective first, and then the ten-year objective is likely to be more realistic and attainable.

Establishing strategic business objectives is especially important if there are separate operating divisions or companies within a group. Without clear objectives for the entire operation there is a risk that the direction will be set by the strongest part of it, and whilst achieving the latter's objectives may be admirable they may not necesssarily be in the best interests of the business as a whole.

- The mission statement is how you want to operate.
- The strategic objective is where you want to go.

B6.2   The Strategic Business Objective

The strategic business objective that we want to reach in *5 years* is:

The strategic business objective that we want to reach in *10 years* is:

■ Form B6.3: The Marketing Objectives

Your marketing objectives are the shorter-term objectives that act as the stepping stones towards the overall strategic objective of the business, organisation or operating division.

Set your three-year objectives first, outline the strategy you will use to achieve them, then establish your five-year objectives. (Note: Because of changing trends or technological developments many producers or service providers do not set their marketing objectives for periods longer than three years).

- The mission statement is how you want to operate.
- The strategic objective is where you want to go.
- The marketing objective is what you want to achieve.

B6.3   The Marketing Objectives

The marketing objectives that we need to achieve
within the next *3 years* in order to maintain progress
towards the strategic business objective are:

The strategy to be adopted is:

The marketing objectives that we need to achieve
within the next *5 years* in order to maintain progress
towards the strategic business objective are:

The strategy to be adopted is:

■ Form B6.4: The Marketing Plan Objectives

With all your medium- and long-term objectives established, the marketing plan is about the tactics you will use in the shorter term (one to two years) to ensure that your more distant objectives can be reached.

But before you can consider deploying resources, people, money and products as part of your tactical planning you will need to establish what you want to achieve at the end of the first year, and possibly also at the end of the second year. So again you need to state your objectives!

Don't forget that within your marketing plan there will be other objectives, such as sales objectives, campaign objectives and so on.

In the third box you should to summarise the key elements needed to ensure your tactical marketing plan succeeds. If for example your objective is to increase sales by 'x' per cent and this can only be achieved by expanding the customer base by 'y' per cent, how are you going to do it? By using media advertising, direct calling or direct mail, or perhaps by taking over a competitor? Once you have decided on your strategy you can consider what resources you are likely to need, whether you already have them or how or where you can obtain them. Summarising your plan will help you identify what's needed.

Do you have the campaign theme and the finances available to achieve your objectives through advertising?

Do you have the sales people for direct calling?

Do you have the database and the brochures to implement an appropriate direct marketing programme?

B6.4   Marketing Plan Objectives and Marketing Plan Summary

The marketing objectives we intend to achieve by the end of years 1 and 2 of the marketing plan are:

Year 1 marketing objective:

Year 2 marketing objective:

The main elements of the marketing plan are summarised as follows:

■ (C) Marketing and Sales Operating Parameters

This section gathers together information relating to:

- Products or services, associated costs and operating margins.

- The sales structure operating areas and costs.

- Marketing and sales costs including marketing communications, advertising costs and sales-force operating costs.

By using the planning forms you can monitor your sales performance by region or salesperson – or both. If you mainly monitor your sales by region, or salesperson, outlet or market segment, use the forms at the beginning of this section. If you monitor your sales by product the forms in the second half of the section will be of more use.

Once you have entered the data for one or other of the above you will find you already have much of the data required for the other part of this section. It will just be a matter of transferring the numbers.

■ Forms C1 and C2: Regional Sales Structure

Form C1: Enter the details of the type of selling structure you have and also the percentage of enquiries and sales each part of the structure deals with.

To provide a measure of selling effectiveness list the number or estimated number of sales enquiries required to achieve each sale. To help put the selling process into a forecast time scale, note the average time from initial enquiry to completion of the sale (invoiced, but not paid) – this could be minutes for a high street retailer or up to a year or more for capital goods sales.

Form C2: Enter the main sales regions in which you operate. These may be the actual regional boundaries of the field salesforce. They may be international or national depending on the type of business you operate.

Sales per region: enter your sales by region for the last two years.

The subregions or areas may be sales territories or catchment areas and subregions by county or town. The main UK regions can be defined by:

- ITV broadcast areas: 15 regions.

- Nielsen index: 13 regions.

- The Registrar General's standard regions of the UK: 11 regions.

For more information on these regions see Chapter 8, 'Targeting'.

C1 Marketing and Sales Operating Parameters: The Selling Structure – Enquiries and Sales

			Percentage of enquiries and sales generated by each sales function			
Tick if applicable		Number employed	% of enquiries generated	% of sales generated	Average number of enquiries per sale	Average time from enquiry to sale
☐	External field sales force (salaried and commission agents)	☐	☐	☐	☐	☐
☐	Internal sales office	☐	☐	☐	☐	☐
☐	Internal order office	☐	☐	☐	☐	☐
☐	Retail sales outlets	☐	☐	☐	☐	☐
☐	Wholesale (inc. cash and carry)	☐	☐	☐	☐	☐
☐	Other	☐	☐	☐	☐	☐

C2 Geographic Regions

The business is divided into the following main geographic regions

Region	Salespeople or outlets per region	Number of subregions	Sales per region for previous two years 19 ... £	19 ... £	Average sales per sales person/outlet in last two years £	£
1						
2						
3						
4						
5						
6						

■ **Form C3: Regional Sales and Sales Costs**

This form summarises by region the yearly selling costs and marketing costs that you have already calculated for each region and salesperson. Make additional copies of this form as required in order to analyse other years.

When this form has been completed you should be in a position to see clearly the selling and marketing costs for each region. The totals in 'surplus towards other costs' can be a useful indicator of regional profitability, especially for fee- and commission-based businesses that do not have high material or purchase costs.

Enter the appropriate £ units (that is, £m, £000s) in the box on the top left-hand side of this form and all subsequent ones with a similar box.

| C3 | Regional Sales and Sales Costs – Yearly Regional Sales Summary |

Units   Year ☐

£ ☐

Regions		Sales	Salaries, commission	Other selling costs	All selling costs	Regional marketing costs	Surplus towards other costs
1	£	☐	☐	☐	☐	☐	☐
	%	☐	☐	☐	☐	☐	☐
2	£	☐	☐	☐	☐	☐	☐
	%	☐	☐	☐	☐	☐	☐
3	£	☐	☐	☐	☐	☐	☐
	%	☐	☐	☐	☐	☐	☐
4	£	☐	☐	☐	☐	☐	☐
	%	☐	☐	☐	☐	☐	☐
5	£	☐	☐	☐	☐	☐	☐
	%	☐	☐	☐	☐	☐	☐
6	£	☐	☐	☐	☐	☐	☐
	%	☐	☐	☐	☐	☐	☐
Totals	£	☐	☐	☐	☐	☐	☐
	=	100%	100%	100%	100%	100%	100%

■ **Forms C3a and C3b: Monthly Regional Sales and Sales Costs**

These forms provide the opportunity to analyse your monthly regional sales and costs.

Transfer the totals on the right-hand side of the form C3a to the sub-total column at the beginning of form C3b.

C3a — All Regions – Monthly Sales and Sales Costs – Months 1–6

Units

£ [   ]   Year ending [   ]

All regions:		1	2	Months 1–6 3	4	5	6	Total months 1–6
Sales	£							
Commission or bonus	£							
Salaries	£							
Other selling costs	£							
Total selling costs	£							
Regional marketing costs	£							
Surplus towards other overheads	£							

C3b — All Regions – Monthly Sales and Sales Costs – Months 7–12

All regions:		Total months 1–6	7	8	Months 7–12 9	10	11	12	Total months 1–12
Sales	£								
Commission or bonus	£								
Salaries	£								
Other selling costs	£								
Total selling costs	£								
Regional marketing costs	£								
Surplus towards other overheads	£								

■ **Forms C3c and C3d: Monthly Sales by Salesperson or Outlet**

Enter the region number (from C2 or C3) and the salesperson's or sales outlet's name in the second box. Enter their monthly sales in months 1–6. If you just want a yearly summary, enter the total yearly figures in box 1.

| C3c | Monthly Sales by Salesperson or Sales Outlet – Months 1–6 |

£ [ ] Year ending [ ]

Units

Region no.	Name		1	2	Months 1–6 3	4	5	6	Total months 1–6
[ ]	[ ]	Sales	[ ]	[ ]	[ ]	[ ]	[ ]	[ ]	[ ]
	All product bonus on sales	[ ] %	[ ]	[ ]	[ ]	[ ]	[ ]	[ ]	[ ]
	Salary	£	[ ]	[ ]	[ ]	[ ]	[ ]	[ ]	[ ]
	Other selling costs	£	[ ]	[ ]	[ ]	[ ]	[ ]	[ ]	[ ]
	Total selling costs	£	[ ]	[ ]	[ ]	[ ]	[ ]	[ ]	[ ]
	% of sales	%	[ ]	[ ]	[ ]	[ ]	[ ]	[ ]	[ ]
[ ]	[ ]	Sales	[ ]	[ ]	[ ]	[ ]	[ ]	[ ]	[ ]
	All product bonus on sales	[ ] %	[ ]	[ ]	[ ]	[ ]	[ ]	[ ]	[ ]
	Salary	£	[ ]	[ ]	[ ]	[ ]	[ ]	[ ]	[ ]
	Other selling costs	£	[ ]	[ ]	[ ]	[ ]	[ ]	[ ]	[ ]
	Total selling costs	£	[ ]	[ ]	[ ]	[ ]	[ ]	[ ]	[ ]
	% of sales	%	[ ]	[ ]	[ ]	[ ]	[ ]	[ ]	[ ]
[ ]	[ ]	Sales	[ ]	[ ]	[ ]	[ ]	[ ]	[ ]	[ ]
	All product bonus on sales	[ ] %	[ ]	[ ]	[ ]	[ ]	[ ]	[ ]	[ ]
	Salary	£	[ ]	[ ]	[ ]	[ ]	[ ]	[ ]	[ ]
	Other selling costs	£	[ ]	[ ]	[ ]	[ ]	[ ]	[ ]	[ ]
	Total selling costs	£	[ ]	[ ]	[ ]	[ ]	[ ]	[ ]	[ ]
	% of sales	%	[ ]	[ ]	[ ]	[ ]	[ ]	[ ]	[ ]

C3d Monthly Sales by Salesperson or Sales Outlet – Months 7–12

£ [ ]   Year ending [ ]

Region no.	Name		Units Total months 1–6	7	8	Months 7–12 9	10	11	12	Total months 1–12
[ ]	[ ]	Sales	[ ]	[ ]	[ ]	[ ]	[ ]	[ ]	[ ]	[ ]
	All product bonus on sales	[ ] %	[ ]	[ ]	[ ]	[ ]	[ ]	[ ]	[ ]	[ ]
	Salary	£	[ ]	[ ]	[ ]	[ ]	[ ]	[ ]	[ ]	[ ]
	Other selling costs	£	[ ]	[ ]	[ ]	[ ]	[ ]	[ ]	[ ]	[ ]
	Total selling costs	£	[ ]	[ ]	[ ]	[ ]	[ ]	[ ]	[ ]	[ ]
	% of sales	%	[ ]	[ ]	[ ]	[ ]	[ ]	[ ]	[ ]	[ ]
[ ]	[ ]	Sales	[ ]	[ ]	[ ]	[ ]	[ ]	[ ]	[ ]	[ ]
	All product bonus on sales	[ ] %	[ ]	[ ]	[ ]	[ ]	[ ]	[ ]	[ ]	[ ]
	Salary	£	[ ]	[ ]	[ ]	[ ]	[ ]	[ ]	[ ]	[ ]
	Other selling costs	£	[ ]	[ ]	[ ]	[ ]	[ ]	[ ]	[ ]	[ ]
	Total selling costs	£	[ ]	[ ]	[ ]	[ ]	[ ]	[ ]	[ ]	[ ]
	% of sales	%	[ ]	[ ]	[ ]	[ ]	[ ]	[ ]	[ ]	[ ]
[ ]	[ ]	Sales	[ ]	[ ]	[ ]	[ ]	[ ]	[ ]	[ ]	[ ]
	All product bonus on sales	[ ] %	[ ]	[ ]	[ ]	[ ]	[ ]	[ ]	[ ]	[ ]
	Salary	£	[ ]	[ ]	[ ]	[ ]	[ ]	[ ]	[ ]	[ ]
	Other selling costs	£	[ ]	[ ]	[ ]	[ ]	[ ]	[ ]	[ ]	[ ]
	Total selling costs	£	[ ]	[ ]	[ ]	[ ]	[ ]	[ ]	[ ]	[ ]
	% of sales	%	[ ]	[ ]	[ ]	[ ]	[ ]	[ ]	[ ]	[ ]

■ **Forms C3e and C3f: Marketing Costs by Region**

You can use these forms to record any marketing expenditure allocated to individual regions. If you wish to record the expenditure of previous years, photocopy these forms. If your marketing expenditure is product-orientated use forms C4d and C4e below.

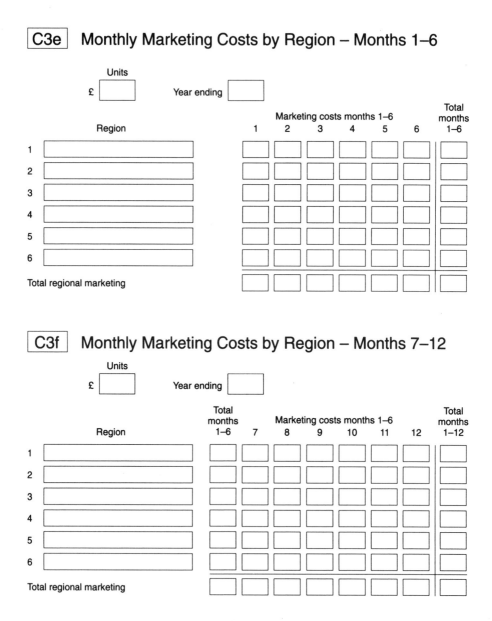

C3e Monthly Marketing Costs by Region – Months 1–6

Units £ [ ]   Year ending [ ]

Region	1	2	3	4	5	6	Total months 1–6
1							
2							
3							
4							
5							
6							
Total regional marketing							

C3f Monthly Marketing Costs by Region – Months 7–12

Units £ [ ]   Year ending [ ]

Region	Total months 1–6	7	8	9	10	11	12	Total months 1–12
1								
2								
3								
4								
5								
6								
Total regional marketing								

■ **Form C4: Products Summary: Sales, Sales Costs and Gross Margin**

If you prefer to monitor your sales and costs by product or product group, forms C4 to C4e will enable you to carry out an in-depth analysis of your sales and contribution by product.

Form C4 summarises the yearly sales, sales costs and marketing costs and contribution that you have already calculated for each product. Make additional copies of this form as required in order to analyse other years.

When the form has been completed you should be able to see clearly what products or services are generating the most profits as well as the marketing support cost of each.

C4 Sales, Sales Costs and Gross Margin by Product

Year

Product or product group		Sales	Materials or purchase costs	Returns/ faulty	Gross margin	Marketing allocation	Contribution to other overheads
A	£						
	%						
B	£						
	%						
C	£						
	%						
D	£						
	%						
E	£						
	%						
F	£						
	%						
Totals	£						
	%	100%	100%	100%	100%	100%	100%

■ Form C4a: Product Sales and Sales Costs

This form summarises data for each product for the previous two years and can be used to improve the accuracy of your sales forecasts by product. Make photocopies and use one sheet for each product or product group.

1. Enter the product code letter and product name as before.

2. Enter information for the previous two years if available.

3. Enter the number of units sold (or the average number of contracts for service business).

4. Enter the selling price. This is your selling price and not necessarily the final selling price.

5. Total sales – multiply the number of units by the price.

6. Enter the unit materials or purchase cost and calculate it as a percentage of sales.

7. Enter an amount per unit for returns and faulty items and calculate it as a percentage of sales.

8. Unit cost of sales – add the amount allocated for returns to the unit material cost and then calculate the value as a percentage of sales.

9. Unit gross margin – this is unit sales minus the unit cost of sales.

10. For total costs of sales, multiply the units total for the year by the unit cost.

11. Enter marketing costs in the same way as above, then calculate the percentages and total costs as above.

12. Unit net contribution towards other costs is unit gross margin minus unit marketing costs. Calculate the percentages and totals as above.

C4a   Product Sales and Sales Costs

Product
code   Name

Enter previous two years' figures

	Year 1	Year 2	Year 1	Year 2

Sales:

Number of units sold   Total sales

Average selling price   £   £   £

Cost of sales:	Cost (£)	%	Cost (£)	%	Cost of sales
Unit materials or purchase cost					£
Average returns and faulty units					£
					Total cost of sales
Cost of sales					£
					Total gross margin
Unit gross margin					£

Allocated marketing costs:	Cost (£)	%	Cost (£)	%	
Advertising and promotion					
Extra quantity discounts					
Free sample allowances					Total allocated marketing costs
Marketing costs per unit					£

% of sales

Total net contribution

Net contribution towards other overheads by unit   £   %   £   %   £

% of sales

■ **Forms C4b and C4c: Product Unit Sales and Net Sales Value**

For each product or product group enter the number of products sold each month, and in the line below enter the net sales value. Copy this form if you want to record sales and marketing costs for previous years. The total figures for the year can be transferred to form C4a, 'Product Sales and Sales Cost', to provide the basis for your product sales cost analysis.

| C4b | Monthly Product Unit Sales and Net Sales Value – Months 1–6 |

Units

£ [   ]   Year ending [   ]

Product/product group		1	2	3	4	5	6	Total months 1–6
A	Unit sales							
	Net sales value (£)							
B	Unit sales							
	Net sales value (£)							
C	Unit sales							
	Net sales value (£)							
D	Unit sales							
	Net sales value (£)							
E	Unit sales							
	Net sales value (£)							
F	Unit sales							
	Net sales value (£)							
Totals	Unit sales							
	Net sales value (£)							

Months 1–6

C4c Monthly Product Unit Sales and Net Sales Value – Months 7–12

Units

£ [   ]

Year ending [   ]

Product/product group		Total months 1–6	Months 7–12						Total months 1–12
			7	8	9	10	11	12	
A [ ]	Unit sales								
	Net sales value (£)								
B [ ]	Unit sales								
	Net sales value (£)								
C [ ]	Unit sales								
	Net sales value (£)								
D [ ]	Unit sales								
	Net sales value (£)								
E [ ]	Unit sales								
	Net sales value (£)								
F [ ]	Unit sales								
	Net sales value (£)								
Totals	Unit sales								
	Net sales value (£)								

■ **Forms C4d and C4e: Marketing Costs by Product**

These are useful forms as they enable you to monitor your marketing expenditure by product group and by month. They are particularly useful if you have individual campaigns for products as you will be able to see clearly the expenditure pattern for each product. For information on previous years photocopy the forms as before.

Transfer your annual total for each product to the relevant copy of form C4a and your monthly totals to the monthly marketing summary forms C5a and C5b.

C4d Monthly Marketing Costs by Product – Months 1–6

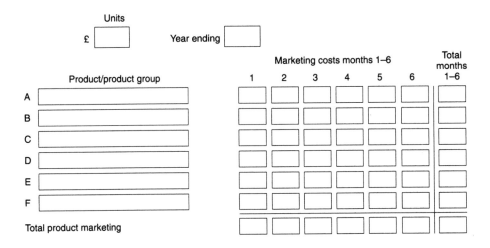

Units

£ ☐   Year ending ☐

| Product/product group | Marketing costs months 1–6 | | | | | | Total months 1–6 |
	1	2	3	4	5	6	
A							
B							
C							
D							
E							
F							
Total product marketing							

C4e Monthly Marketing Costs by Product – Months 7–12

Units

£ ☐   Year ending ☐

| Product/product group | Total months 1–6 | Marketing costs months 7–12 | | | | | | Total months 1–12 |
		7	8	9	10	11	12	
A								
B								
C								
D								
E								
F								
Total product marketing								

■ **Form C5: Marketing Cost Summary**

This form enables you to list all your marketing costs on one sheet. The summary totals can be obtained from the year-end figures you will arrive at when you have completed your analysis of monthly marketing costs on forms C5a and C5b below.

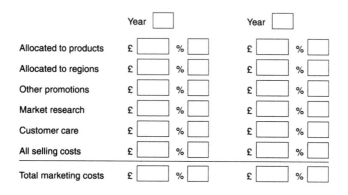

■ **Forms C5a and C5b: Monthly Marketing Costs**

These two forms summarise your marketing expenditure by month as well as helping to identify areas of over- or under-expenditure. The information provides a very useful background from which to develop future marketing budgets and forecasts of future expenditure.

1. Allocated to product: transfer these figures from the monthly all-product expenditure totals on forms C4d and C4e above.

2. Allocated to all regions: transfer these monthly figures from the monthly all regions totals on forms C3a and C3b above.

3. Other promotions: this is expenditure that has not been allocated to any other area.

4. Market Research: if applicable these costs are entered in the box for the month in which the work was completed.

5. Customer Care: if applicable these costs are entered as they occur.

6. All selling costs: these monthly figures are taken from the monthly all-region totals on forms C3a and C3 above.

C5a Monthly Marketing Costs – Months 1–6

C5b Monthly Marketing Costs – Months 7–12

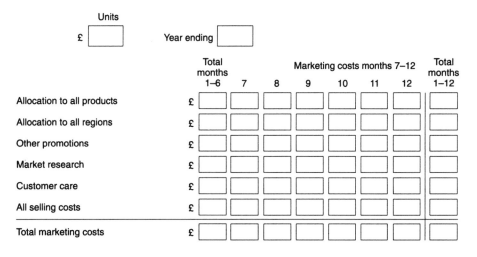

■ (D) Global Overheads and Contributions

All the sales and costs entered in this section are all historic and most of them are in a similar order to your management or annual accounts.

■ Form D1: Global Overheads and Contributions

Enter the figures for the past two years on this form. This data will provide much of the background information you will need to produce accurate forecasts.

1. Sales and cost of sales: these figures can be transferred from the totals on the product summary form C4 above.

2. Gross margins: subtract cost of sales from sales above.

3. Marketing and selling costs: transfer these figures from form C5 above.

4. Contribution to other overheads: deduct marketing costs from the gross margin figure above.

5. Establishment costs, administration costs, wages and salaries, financial and professional fees: these figures can be obtained from the annual totals on form – D1 below.

D1   Global Overheads and Contributions – Annual Sales, Costs and Pretax Profits

	Units	Year 1		Year 2	
	£ [ ]	[ ]		[ ]	
Sales		£ [ ]		£ [ ]	
Cost of sales		£ [ ]	% [ ]	£ [ ]	% [ ]
Gross margin		£ [ ]	% [ ]	£ [ ]	% [ ]
Marketing and selling costs		£ [ ]	% [ ]	£ [ ]	% [ ]
Contribution to other overheads		£ [ ]	% [ ]	£ [ ]	% [ ]
Establishment costs		£ [ ]	% [ ]	£ [ ]	% [ ]
Administration costs		£ [ ]	% [ ]	£ [ ]	% [ ]
Wages and salaries		£ [ ]	% [ ]	£ [ ]	% [ ]
Financial and professional fees		£ [ ]	% [ ]	£ [ ]	% [ ]
Profit before tax and distributions		£ [ ]	% [ ]	£ [ ]	% [ ]

■ Forms D1a, D1b and D1c

Form D1a will enable you to analyse monthly profitability and D1b and D1c monthly overhead expenditure.

For ease of analysis on forms D1b and D1c overhead subheadings have been grouped into subsections. Transfer the monthly section totals from these forms to the appropriate month in the Passive Costs section on form D1a.

To calculate your monthly profit, enter on D1a monthly sales totals either from forms C3a and C3b for sales persons or sales regions totals, or C4a and C4b for monthly product sales.

The gross margin is calculated by deducting the cost of sales from the monthly sales figure. For regional or salesperson sales this monthly cost of sales is transferred from the previously calculated Total Selling Costs on forms C3a and C3b.

For products the monthly cost of sales is calculated by adding together Total Cost of Sales figure from form C4a for each product and dividing the total by twelve to obtain the monthly average. The gross margin is calculated by adding together the Total Gross Margin figures for each product, also from form C4a, and dividing the total by twelve to obtain the monthly average.

The marketing costs are transferred from the monthly totals on forms C5a and C5b. Deducting these figures from the monthly Gross Margin provides the operating profit or contribution towards other overheads. Subtracting the Passive Cost subtotals already entered from D1b and D1c provides the monthly profit (or loss) figure which is entered in the profit before tax box.

Don't forget to spread the cost of large items of expenditure such as bulk purchases, brochures, direct mail costs, rates or insurance over the appropriate time scale otherwise the monthly contibution and the profit before tax figures could be distorted and may not accurately reflect profit trends.

D1a Monthly Costs and Pretax Profits

Units
£ [   ]   Year ending [   ]

	£	Months 1–6						Total months 1–6
		1	2	3	4	5	6	
Sales	£							
Cost of sales	£							
Gross margin	£							
Marketing costs	£							
Contribute to other o/h	£							

Passive costs:

	£	1	2	3	4	5	6	
Establishment	£							
Administration costs	£							
Wages and salaries	£							
Finance/professional	£							
Profit before tax and distributions	£							

	£	Total months 1–6	Months 7–12						Total months 1–12
			7	8	9	10	11	12	
Sales	£								
Cost of sales	£								
Gross margin	£								
Marketing costs	£								
Contribute to other o/h	£								

Passive costs:

	£	Total months 1–6	7	8	9	10	11	12	Total months 1–12
Establishment	£								
Administration costs	£								
Wages and salaries	£								
Finance/professional	£								
Profit before tax and distributions	£								

D1b   Establish Financial and Other Overhead Costs – Months 1–6

Units

£ [   ]   Year ending [   ]

Establishment:		1	2	3	4	5	6	Total months 1–6
Rent	£							
Rates and water	£							
Lighting and heating	£							
Power	£							
Repair and maintenance	£							
Insurances	£							
Depreciation	£							
Health and safety	£							
Sundries	£							
Total establishment	£							
Administration:								
Office stationery	£							
Office equipment	£							
Telephone	£							
Postage	£							
Training	£							
Motor expenses	£							
Travel/entertainment	£							
Other	£							
Total administration	£							
Total wages and salaries	£							
Financial/professional:								
Audit/accountancy	£							
Legal fees	£							
Bank charges & interest	£							
Lease charges & interest	£							
HP charges & interest	£							
Other	£							
Total financial/professional	£							
Total passive costs	£							

D1c Establish Financial and Other Overhead Costs – Months 7–12

Units

£ [ ]   Year ending [ ]

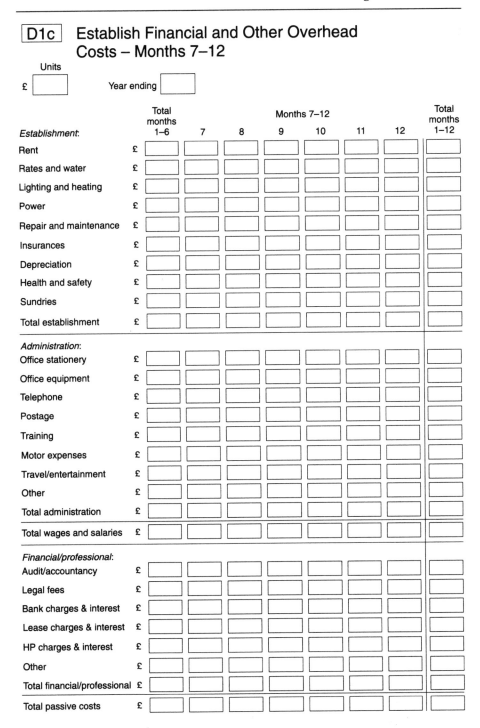

Establishment:		Total months 1–6	7	8	9	10	11	12	Total months 1–12
Rent	£								
Rates and water	£								
Lighting and heating	£								
Power	£								
Repair and maintenance	£								
Insurances	£								
Depreciation	£								
Health and safety	£								
Sundries	£								
Total establishment	£								
Administration:									
Office stationery	£								
Office equipment	£								
Telephone	£								
Postage	£								
Training	£								
Motor expenses	£								
Travel/entertainment	£								
Other	£								
Total administration	£								
Total wages and salaries	£								
Financial/professional:									
Audit/accountancy	£								
Legal fees	£								
Bank charges & interest	£								
Lease charges & interest	£								
HP charges & interest	£								
Other	£								
Total financial/professional	£								
Total passive costs	£								

Months 7–12

■ (E) Profit and Loss Forecasting

In this section you will prepare your forecasts of future revenue, expenditure and profit. The form layouts and subheadings in this section are virtually identical to their counterparts in Sections C and D.

The most important choice to make before starting your forecast is to decide what is most important to your business. Do you want to forecast by product/product group, by region, by outlet or by salesperson?

■ Form E1: Annual Pretax Sales, Costs and Profits

This is the five-year summary forecast of all your future financial expectations. The subheadings are the same as those in Section D. You can obtain the summary totals from the totals you will calculate on forms E1a–E1f.

Work on your first year's monthly sales forecasts first, from the lowest level possible – that is, sales by product or by salesperson – and then build up your forecasts, adding marketing and selling costs where appropriate.

E1 Annual Forecast of Sales, Costs and Pretax Profits (5 Years)

	Years				
Units	1	2	3	4	5
£ [ ]					
Sales £					
Cost of sales £					
%					
Gross margin £					
%					
Marketing and selling costs £					
%					
Contribution to other overheads £					
%					
Establishment costs £					
%					
Administration costs £					
%					
Wages and salaries £					
%					
Financial and professional fees £					
%					
Profit before tax and distributions £					
%					

■   **Forms E1a–E1d: Monthly Sales and Profit Forecasts – 1st Year**

These forms allow you to summarise your total sales and profit forecasts by month.

E1a   Monthly Forecast Sales, Costs and Profits – Months 1–6

Units

£ [   ]   Year ending [   ]

		1	2	Months 1–6 3	4	5	6	Total months 1–6
Sales	£							
Cost of sales	£							
Gross margin	£							
Marketing costs	£							
Contribute to other o/h	£							
Passive costs:								
Establishment	£							
Administration costs	£							
Wages and salaries	£							
Financial/professional	£							
Profit before tax and distributions	£							

E1b Monthly Forecast Sales, Costs and Profits – Months 7–12

Units
£ [　　　]   Year ending [　　　]

		Total months 1–6	7	8	Months 7–12 9	10	11	12	Total months 1–12
Sales	£								
Cost of sales	£								
Gross margin	£								
Marketing costs	£								
Contribute to other o/h	£								
Passive costs:									
Establishment	£								
Administration costs	£								
Wages and salaries	£								
Financial/professional	£								
Profit before tax and distributions	£								

E1c Monthly Forecast Sales, Costs and Profits – Months 13–18

Units
£ [　　　]   Year ending [　　　]

		Total months 1–12	13	14	Months 13–18 15	16	17	18	Total months 1–18
Sales	£								
Cost of sales	£								
Gross margin	£								
Marketing costs	£								
Contribute to other o/h	£								
Passive costs:									
Establishment	£								
Administration costs	£								
Wages and salaries	£								
Financial/professional	£								
Profit before tax and distributions	£								

E1d Monthly Forecast Sales, Costs and Profits – Months 19–24

Units

£ [   ]   Year ending [   ]

		Total months 1–18	19	20	Months 19–24 21	Months 19–24 22	23	24	Total months 1–24
Sales	£								
Cost of sales	£								
Gross margin	£								
Marketing costs	£								
Contribute to other o/h	£								
Passive costs:									
Establishment	£								
Administration costs	£								
Wages and salaries	£								
Financial/professional	£								
Profit before tax and distributions	£								

■ Forms E1e and E1f: Forecast of Overheads

Because most overhead costs are easier to predict than sales revenues and sales costs, overheads should be calculated separately and the totals carried forward to the summary sheet.

With this plan you can produce a two-year monthly profit- and loss-forecast and a one-year cash flow forecast (see Section F). We consider that this should be sufficient for almost all purposes, but if further years are required additional sheets can be photocopied.

Transfer the end-of-year totals from the monthly sheets to the appropriate boxes for years one and two. Using these two years as a guide, you can now complete the five-year forecast (form E1).

E1e   Establish Financial and Other Overhead Costs – Months 1–6

Units

£ [ ]   Year ending [ ]

Establishment:		1	2	3	4	5	6	Total months 1–6
Rent	£							
Rates and water	£							
Lighting and heating	£							
Power	£							
Repair and maintenance	£							
Insurances	£							
Depreciation	£							
Health and safety	£							
Sundries	£							
Total establishment	£							
Administration:								
Office stationery	£							
Office equipment	£							
Telephone	£							
Postage	£							
Training	£							
Motor expenses	£							
Travel/entertainment	£							
Other	£							
Total administration	£							
Total wages and salaries	£							
Financial/professional:								
Audit/accountancy	£							
Legal fees	£							
Bank charges & interest	£							
Lease charges & interest	£							
HP charges & interest	£							
Other	£							
Total financial/professional	£							
Total passive costs	£							

Months 1–6

E1f   Establish Financial and Other Overhead Costs – Months 7–12

Units

£ [　　　]   Year ending [　　　]

Establishment:		Total months 1–6	7	8	9	10	11	12	Total months 1–12
Rent	£								
Rates and water	£								
Lighting and heating	£								
Power	£								
Repair and maintenance	£								
Insurances	£								
Depreciation	£								
Health and safety	£								
Sundries	£								
Total establishment	£								
Administration:									
Office stationery	£								
Office equipment	£								
Telephone	£								
Postage	£								
Training	£								
Motor expenses	£								
Travel/entertainment	£								
Other	£								
Total administration	£								
Total wages and salaries	£								
Financial/professional:									
Audit/accountancy	£								
Legal fees	£								
Bank charges & interest	£								
Lease charges & interest	£								
HP charges & interest	£								
Other	£								
Total financial/professional	£								
Total passive costs	£								

■ **Form E2: Forecast Trading Asset Statement**

You are in business to make a living and create some wealth for yourself, and your success in the latter endeavour will show in an improvement in the balance sheet between the beginning and the end of the year.

The balance sheet summarises both increases and decreases in fixed assets such as land, buildings or machinery, and as well as 'liquid' or 'trading' assets and liabilities such as stock, debtors, trade creditors and overdrafts or loans used to provide working capital.

The value of fixed assets can vary tremendously between businesses, even among direct competitors with similar turnovers. For example some businesses may prefer to rent premises or equipment, some may prefer to buy; some may have been trading for many years and have paid off all their mortgages or loans on fixed assets, others may have just started to purchase or instead have invested their surplus profits in other ventures.

Whilst many businesses make profits on their fixed assets or investments, the true measure of business success is an increase in the net liquid assets that are generated from trading profits.

The net worth of the business is the difference between assets and liabilities, but because of the above and because this planning process focuses on sales or trading activity we have excluded fixed assets such as land, buildings and machinery from the yearly summary and concentrated on producing a statement of net worth in the form of a 'trading asset statement' based on current assets and liabilities, as we consider these to be the items that affect the health of your business.

Trading assets are items such as stock, debtors and cash at the bank and a forecast of their value can be produced by using the following calculation:

- Stock: calculated as the average number of months sales that are held as stock.

- Debtors: calculated as average debtor days times total sales divided by 365.

- Cash at bank: this would be estimated as the sum of any positive bank balance at the start of the forecast period plus any other cash deposits.

Trading liabilities are items such as trade creditors, other creditors including VAT and National Insurance contributions, overdrafts and bank loans.

- Trade creditors: calculated as the average payment period in days times total cost of sales divided by 365.

- Other creditor: calculated as overheads times 'days of grace' you take to pay (i.e. 30 days) divided by 365.

- Overdrafts: the amount that the business is overdrawn on its trading bank accounts at the start of the forecast period.

- Short-term loans and other borrowings: these are the balances at the start of the period on loans and other short term borrowings (excluding overdrafts) used for trading purposes.

Long-term debtors such as mortgages and loans over five years are ignored.

If you want to prepare a conventional balance sheet for any of the forecast years, just merge the figures produced by this forecast with your forecasts of fixed asset movement, long-term liabilities, tax, owners' funds and so on, on a separate sheet using your usual balance sheet layout and standard accounting principles.

You will not be able to complete the future years columns in the forecast trading asset statement until you have prepared your forecast of sales, profits and overheads and completed the cash flow calculations in Section F.

E2 Yearly Forecast Trading Asset Statement

Units

£ [   ]

Year ending [   ]

	Opening position	Years 1	2	3	4	5
(A) Trading assets						
Stock						
Debtors						
Cash						
Total						
(B) Trading liabilities						
Trade creditors						
Other creditors						
Loans & other borrowing for trading purpose only						
Total						
(C) Net trading asset position (A–B)						
(D) Change from previous year (+/–)						

■ Form E3: Regional Sales and Sales Costs

This form summarises by region the annual selling costs and marketing costs that you have already forecast for each region and salesperson. Make additional copies of this form as required in order to analyse other years.

When this form has been completed you should be in a position to see clearly the selling and marketing costs for each region. The totals in 'surplus available towards other costs' can be a useful indicator of regional profitability, especially for fee- and commission-based businesses that do not have high material or purchase costs in their sales figures.

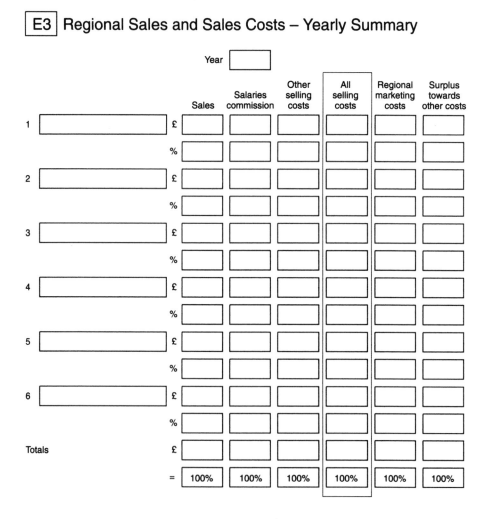

| E3 | Regional Sales and Sales Costs – Yearly Summary |

■ **Forms E3a–E3d: Monthly Regional Sales and Sales Costs; and Forms E3e–E3h: Monthly Marketing Costs by Region**

These forms provide the opportunity to forecast your regional sales and costs by month. Add up the first six months for each row and transfer the totals to the column at the beginning of the second form.

If you allocate your marketing budgets by region, enter the monthly amounts or totals on the appropriate form.

E3a All Regions – Monthly Sales and Sales Costs – Months 1–6

Units

£ [ ]   Year ending [ ]

All regions:		Months 1–6						Total months 1–6
		1	2	3	4	5	6	
Sales	£	[ ]	[ ]	[ ]	[ ]	[ ]	[ ]	[ ]
Commission or bonus	£	[ ]	[ ]	[ ]	[ ]	[ ]	[ ]	[ ]
Salaries	£	[ ]	[ ]	[ ]	[ ]	[ ]	[ ]	[ ]
Other selling costs	£	[ ]	[ ]	[ ]	[ ]	[ ]	[ ]	[ ]
Total selling costs	£	[ ]	[ ]	[ ]	[ ]	[ ]	[ ]	[ ]
Regional marketing costs	£	[ ]	[ ]	[ ]	[ ]	[ ]	[ ]	[ ]
Surplus towards other overheads	£	[ ]	[ ]	[ ]	[ ]	[ ]	[ ]	[ ]

E3b   All Regions – Monthly Sales and Sales Costs – Months 7–12

All regions:		Total months 1–6	Months 7–12						Total months 1–12
			1	2	3	4	5	6	
Sales	£								
Commission or bonus	£								
Salaries	£								
Other selling costs	£								
Total selling costs	£								
Regional marketing costs	£								
Surplus towards other overheads	£								

E3c   All Regions – Monthly Sales and Sales Costs – Months 13–18

All regions:		Total months 1–12	Months 13–18						Total months 1–18
			13	14	15	16	17	18	
Sales	£								
Commission or bonus	£								
Salaries	£								
Other selling costs	£								
Total selling costs	£								
Regional marketing costs	£								
Surplus towards other overheads	£								

E3d All Regions – Monthly Sales and Sales Costs – Months 19–24

All regions:		Total months 1–18	19	20	21	22	23	24	Total months 1–24
					Months 19–24				
Sales	£								
Commission or bonus	£								
Salaries	£								
Other selling costs	£								
Total selling costs	£								
Regional marketing costs	£								
Surplus towards other overheads	£								

E3e Monthly Marketing Costs by Region – Months 1–6

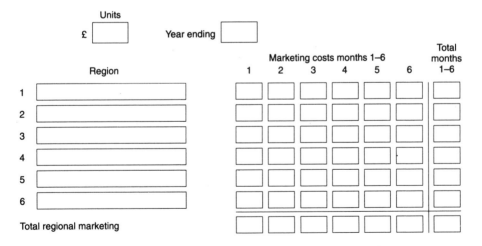

Units £ [ ]   Year ending [ ]

Region		1	2	3	4	5	6	Total months 1–6
				Marketing costs months 1–6				
1								
2								
3								
4								
5								
6								
Total regional marketing								

E3f   Monthly Marketing Costs by Region – Months 7–12

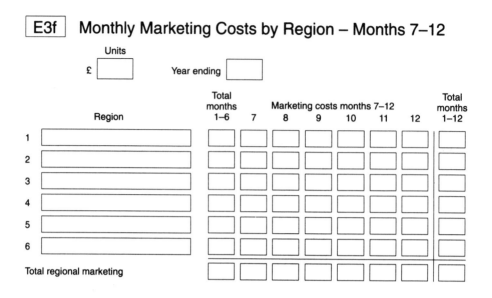

Units

£ [   ]   Year ending [   ]

Region	Total months 1–6	7	8	9	10	11	12	Total months 1–12
1								
2								
3								
4								
5								
6								
Total regional marketing								

(Marketing costs months 7–12)

E3g   Monthly Marketing Costs by Region – Months 13–18

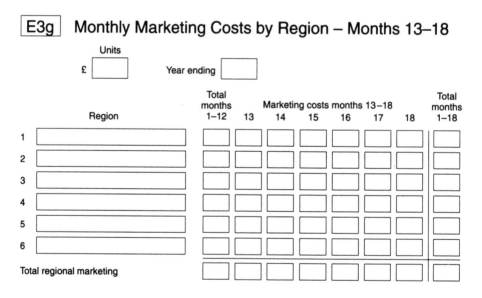

Units

£ [   ]   Year ending [   ]

Region	Total months 1–12	13	14	15	16	17	18	Total months 1–18
1								
2								
3								
4								
5								
6								
Total regional marketing								

(Marketing costs months 13–18)

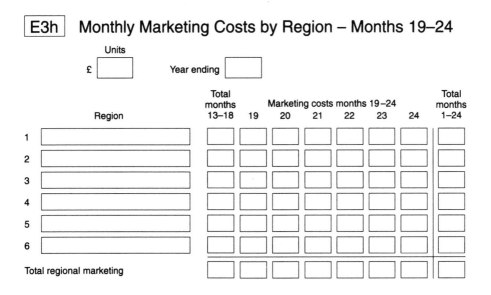

| E3h | Monthly Marketing Costs by Region – Months 19–24 |

Units

£ [ ]   Year ending [ ]

Region	Total months 13–18	19	20	21	22	23	24	Total months 1–24
1								
2								
3								
4								
5								
6								
Total regional marketing								

(Marketing costs months 19–24)

■ **Forms E3i and E3j: Monthly Sales by Salesperson or Outlet**

Enter the region number (from form C1 or C3) and the salesperson's or sales outlet's name in the second box. Enter your monthly sales in months 1–6. If you just want annual forecasts, enter the total yearly figures in box 1.

E3i	Monthly Sales by Salesperson or Sales Outlet – Months 1–6

£ [   ]   Year ending [   ]

Units

Region no.	Name		1	2	3	4	5	6	Total months 1–6
[ ]	[ ]	Sales	[ ]	[ ]	[ ]	[ ]	[ ]	[ ]	[ ]
	All product bonus on sales	[ ] %	[ ]	[ ]	[ ]	[ ]	[ ]	[ ]	[ ]
	Salary	£	[ ]	[ ]	[ ]	[ ]	[ ]	[ ]	[ ]
	Other selling costs	£	[ ]	[ ]	[ ]	[ ]	[ ]	[ ]	[ ]
	Total selling costs	£	[ ]	[ ]	[ ]	[ ]	[ ]	[ ]	[ ]
	% of sales	%	[ ]	[ ]	[ ]	[ ]	[ ]	[ ]	[ ]
[ ]	[ ]	Sales	[ ]	[ ]	[ ]	[ ]	[ ]	[ ]	[ ]
	All product bonus on sales	[ ] %	[ ]	[ ]	[ ]	[ ]	[ ]	[ ]	[ ]
	Salary	£	[ ]	[ ]	[ ]	[ ]	[ ]	[ ]	[ ]
	Other selling costs	£	[ ]	[ ]	[ ]	[ ]	[ ]	[ ]	[ ]
	Total selling costs	£	[ ]	[ ]	[ ]	[ ]	[ ]	[ ]	[ ]
	% of sales	%	[ ]	[ ]	[ ]	[ ]	[ ]	[ ]	[ ]
[ ]	[ ]	Sales	[ ]	[ ]	[ ]	[ ]	[ ]	[ ]	[ ]
	All product bonus on sales	[ ] %	[ ]	[ ]	[ ]	[ ]	[ ]	[ ]	[ ]
	Salary	£	[ ]	[ ]	[ ]	[ ]	[ ]	[ ]	[ ]
	Other selling costs	£	[ ]	[ ]	[ ]	[ ]	[ ]	[ ]	[ ]
	Total selling costs	£	[ ]	[ ]	[ ]	[ ]	[ ]	[ ]	[ ]
	% of sales	%	[ ]	[ ]	[ ]	[ ]	[ ]	[ ]	[ ]

E3j Monthly Sales by Salesperson or Sales Outlet – Months 7–12

£ [ ] Year ending [ ]

Region no.	Name	Units	Total months 1–6	7	8	Months 7–12 9	10	11	12	Total months 1–12
[ ]	[ ]	Sales								
	All product bonus on sales	[ ] %								
	Salary	£								
	Other selling costs	£								
	Total selling costs	£								
	% of sales	%								
[ ]	[ ]	Sales								
	All product bonus on sales	[ ] %								
	Salary	£								
	Other selling costs	£								
	Total selling costs	£								
	% of sales	%								
[ ]	[ ]	Sales								
	All product bonus on sales	[ ] %								
	Salary	£								
	Other selling costs	£								
	Total selling costs	£								
	% of sales	%								

■ **Form E4: Products Summary: Sales, Sales Costs and Gross Margin**

This form summarises the yearly sales, sales costs, marketing costs and contribution that you have forecast for each product. Make additional copies of this form as required in order to forecast other years. When you have completed this form you should be in a position to see clearly what products or services are generating the most profits and the marketing support cost of each of them.

E4 Sales, Sales Costs and Gross Margin by Product

Year ☐

Product or product group		Sales	Materials or purchase costs	Returns/ faulty	Gross margin	Marketing allocation	Contribution to other overheads
A	£						
	%						
B	£						
	%						
C	£						
	%						
D	£						
	%						
E	£						
	%						
F	£						
	%						
Totals	£						
	%	100%	100%	100%	100%	100%	100%

■ Form E4a: Product Sales and Sales Costs

This form is almost the same as the one completed in Section C (form C4a). The main differences are that the objective is forecasting and the years to be entered at the top of each column are for the next two forecast years. Use one sheet for each product or product group.

1. Enter the first and second years of your forecast period.

2. Enter the product code letter and product name as before.

3. Transfer the number of units sold (or the average number of contracts for service business).

4. Enter the selling price. This is your selling price, and not necessarily the final selling price.

5. Total sales: simply multiply the units by the price.

6. Enter the unit materials or purchase cost and calculate it as a percentage of sales.

7. Enter an amount per unit for returns and faulty items and calculate it as a percentage of sales.

8. Unit cost of sales: add the amount allocated for returns to the unit material costs and then calculate the value as a percentage of sales.

9. Unit gross margin: this is unit sales minus unit cost of sales.

10. Total costs of sales: multiply the unit total for the year by the unit cost.

11. Enter marketing costs in the same way as above, calculate percentages and total costs as above.

12. Unit net contribution towards other costs is unit gross margin less unit marketing costs. Calculate the percentages and totals as above.

E4a Product Sales and Sales Costs

Product code

Name

Enter previous two years' figures

	Year 1	Year 2	Year 1	Year 2

Sales:

Number of units sold

Average selling price   £   £   £

Total sales

Cost of sales: Cost (£)   %   Cost (£)   %   Cost of sales

Unit materials or purchase cost   £

Average returns and faulty units   £

Total cost of sales

Cost of sales   £

Total gross margin

Unit gross margin   £

Allocated marketing and sales costs: Cost (£)   %   Cost (£)   %

Advertising and promotion

Extra quantity discounts

Free sample allowances

Demonstration allowances and others

Marketing costs per unit

Total allocated marketing costs
£

% of sales

Total net contribution

Net contribution towards other overheads by unit   £   %   £   %   £

% of sales

■ **Forms E4b and E4c: Product Unit Sales and Net Sales Value**

For each product or product group enter the number of products sold each month, and in the line below the next sales value. The total figures for the year can be transferred to form E4a above to provide the basis for your product sales cost analysis.

E4b	Monthly Product Unit Sales and Net Sales Value – Months 1–6

Units

£ [　　] Year ending [　　]

Product/product group		1	2	3	4	5	6	Total months 1–6
A	Unit sales							
Average unit value	Net sales value (£)							
B	Unit sales							
Average unit value	Net sales value (£)							
C	Unit sales							
Average unit value	Net sales value (£)							
D	Unit sales							
Average unit value	Net sales value (£)							
E	Unit sales							
Average unit value	Net sales value (£)							
F	Unit sales							
Average unit value	Net sales value (£)							
Totals	Unit sales							
	Net sales value (£)							

Months 1–6

E4c | Monthly Product Unit Sales and Net Sales Value – Months 7–12

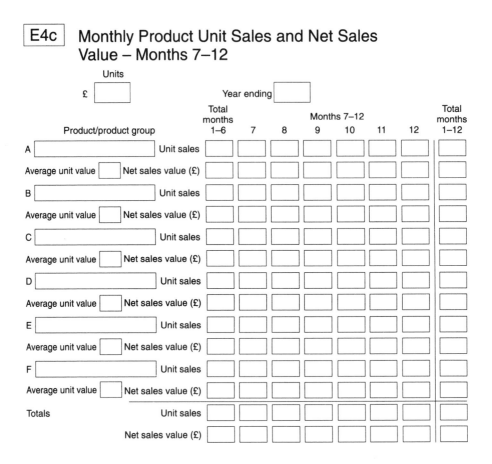

Product/product group	Total months 1–6	7	8	9	10	11	12	Total months 1–12
A _____ Unit sales								
Average unit value ___ Net sales value (£)								
B _____ Unit sales								
Average unit value ___ Net sales value (£)								
C _____ Unit sales								
Average unit value ___ Net sales value (£)								
D _____ Unit sales								
Average unit value ___ Net sales value (£)								
E _____ Unit sales								
Average unit value ___ Net sales value (£)								
F _____ Unit sales								
Average unit value ___ Net sales value (£)								
Totals Unit sales								
Net sales value (£)								

Units £ _____   Year ending _____   Months 7–12

■ **Forms E4d and E4e: Marketing Costs by Product**

These are useful forms as they enable you to monitor your marketing costs by product and by month. They also enable you to monitor your marketing expenditure by product group and by month, which is particularly useful if you have individual campaigns for different products as you will be able to see clearly the expenditure pattern for each product.

Transfer the annual total for each product to the relevant copy of form E4a and your monthly totals to marketing monthly summary forms E5a and E5b below.

To prepare year-two forecasts photocopy the above forms.

E4d Monthly Marketing Costs by Product – Months 1–6

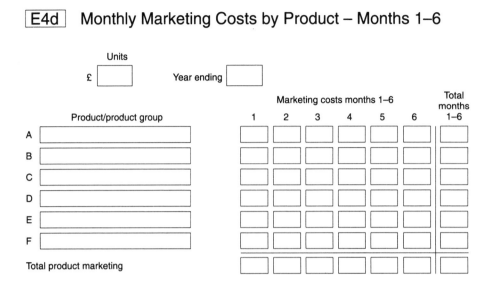

	Product/product group	1	2	3	4	5	6	Total months 1–6
A								
B								
C								
D								
E								
F								
Total product marketing								

Units £ [ ] Year ending [ ]

Marketing costs months 1–6

E4e Monthly Marketing Costs by Product – Months 7–12

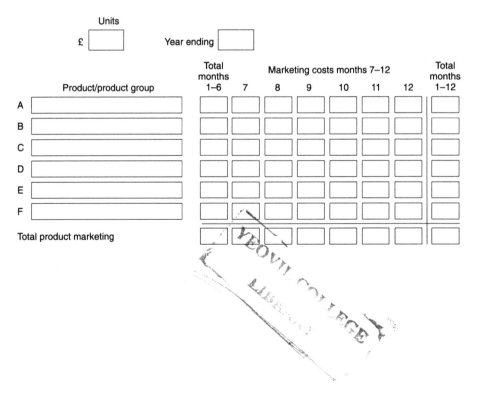

Units £ [ ] Year ending [ ]

	Product/product group	Total months 1–6	7	8	9	10	11	12	Total months 1–12
A									
B									
C									
D									
E									
F									
Total product marketing									

Marketing costs months 7–12

■ **Form E5: Marketing Budget Summary**

On this form enter your forecast of marketing expenditure for the next five years.

E5   Marketing Budget Summary – 5 Year Forecast of Marketing Costs

Units

£ [   ]

	Years				
	1	2	3	4	5
	[ ]	[ ]	[ ]	[ ]	[ ]
Allocation to all products	£ [ ]	£ [ ]	£ [ ]	£ [ ]	£ [ ]
	% [ ]	% [ ]	% [ ]	% [ ]	% [ ]
Allocation to all regions	£ [ ]	£ [ ]	£ [ ]	£ [ ]	£ [ ]
	% [ ]	% [ ]	% [ ]	% [ ]	% [ ]
Other promotions	£ [ ]	£ [ ]	£ [ ]	£ [ ]	£ [ ]
	% [ ]	% [ ]	% [ ]	% [ ]	% [ ]
Market research	£ [ ]	£ [ ]	£ [ ]	£ [ ]	£ [ ]
	% [ ]	% [ ]	% [ ]	% [ ]	% [ ]
Customer care	£ [ ]	£ [ ]	£ [ ]	£ [ ]	£ [ ]
	% [ ]	% [ ]	% [ ]	% [ ]	% [ ]
All selling costs	£ [ ]	£ [ ]	£ [ ]	£ [ ]	£ [ ]
	% [ ]	% [ ]	% [ ]	% [ ]	% [ ]
Total marketing costs	£ [ ]	£ [ ]	£ [ ]	£ [ ]	£ [ ]
	% [ ]	% [ ]	% [ ]	% [ ]	% [ ]

■ **Forms E5a–E5d: Monthly Marketing Budgets**

These four forms enable you to forecast your monthly marketing budgets for two years (you will need a photocopy of forms E5q and E5b for the second year. You only have to consider any likely monthly expenditure on 'other promotions', 'market research' and 'customer care'. Calculate all percentages as a percentage of 'total marketing costs'.

E5a | Monthly Marketing Costs – Months 1–6

Units

£ [ ]   Year ending [ ]

All regions:		Months 1–6						Total months 1–6
		1	2	3	4	5	6	
Allocation to all products	£							
Allocation to all regions	£							
Other promotions	£							
Market research	£							
Customer care	£							
All selling costs	£							
Total marketing costs	£							

E5b | Monthly Marketing Costs – Months 7–12

Units

£ [ ]   Year ending [ ]

All regions:		Total months 1–6	Months 7–12						Total months 1–12
			7	8	9	10	11	12	
Allocation to all products	£								
Allocation to all regions	£								
Other promotions	£								
Market research	£								
Customer care	£								
All selling costs	£								
Total marketing costs	£								

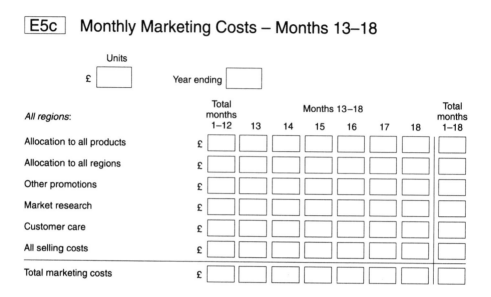

E5c   Monthly Marketing Costs – Months 13–18

Units

£ [ ]   Year ending [ ]

All regions:		Total months 1–12	Months 13–18						Total months 1–18
			13	14	15	16	17	18	
Allocation to all products	£	[ ]	[ ]	[ ]	[ ]	[ ]	[ ]	[ ]	[ ]
Allocation to all regions	£	[ ]	[ ]	[ ]	[ ]	[ ]	[ ]	[ ]	[ ]
Other promotions	£	[ ]	[ ]	[ ]	[ ]	[ ]	[ ]	[ ]	[ ]
Market research	£	[ ]	[ ]	[ ]	[ ]	[ ]	[ ]	[ ]	[ ]
Customer care	£	[ ]	[ ]	[ ]	[ ]	[ ]	[ ]	[ ]	[ ]
All selling costs	£	[ ]	[ ]	[ ]	[ ]	[ ]	[ ]	[ ]	[ ]
Total marketing costs	£	[ ]	[ ]	[ ]	[ ]	[ ]	[ ]	[ ]	[ ]

E5d   Monthly Marketing Costs – Months 19–24

Units

£ [ ]   Year ending [ ]

All regions:		Total months 1–18	Months 19–24						Total months 1–24
			19	20	21	22	23	24	
Allocation to all products	£	[ ]	[ ]	[ ]	[ ]	[ ]	[ ]	[ ]	[ ]
Allocation to all regions	£	[ ]	[ ]	[ ]	[ ]	[ ]	[ ]	[ ]	[ ]
Other promotions	£	[ ]	[ ]	[ ]	[ ]	[ ]	[ ]	[ ]	[ ]
Market research	£	[ ]	[ ]	[ ]	[ ]	[ ]	[ ]	[ ]	[ ]
Customer care	£	[ ]	[ ]	[ ]	[ ]	[ ]	[ ]	[ ]	[ ]
All selling costs	£	[ ]	[ ]	[ ]	[ ]	[ ]	[ ]	[ ]	[ ]
Total marketing costs	£	[ ]	[ ]	[ ]	[ ]	[ ]	[ ]	[ ]	[ ]

■ (F) Cash Flow Forecasting

Although cash flow forecasting is not traditionally considered to be an integral part of marketing, without a regular cash flow no business or organisation can survive for long.

The forms in this section are designed to help you forecast your revenue inflows and outflows for twelve months. If you wish to forecast for a longer period, photocopy the forms.

If you are not registered for VAT or operate a VAT-exempt business or organisation, delete 'ex-VAT' from the summary sheet, ignore the VAT balance forms F1c and F1d and enter all appropriate expenditure as VAT inclusive.

■ Forms F1a and F1b: Monthly Net Revenue Inflow/Outflow

Completing these two forms will show you how your cash requirement is likely to fluctuate during the forecast period. Knowing the variation should help you to plan your cash management.

If your forecast indicates that you need more funds than are available, you can make arrangements to fill the gap. If on the other hand your forecast indicates you are going to produce a surplus, you can consider how to make this surplus work for you.

Form F1a: *Numbers 1 and 2*: From each of the monthly totals of revenue inflow on Form F2a further on in this section, calculate (if applicable) the percentage of revenue that includes VAT. Deduct the VAT from each month's figure and enter the revenue (excluding VAT) on the first line of form F1a. Enter zero rated or other non-VAT revenue in line 2.

Enter the calculated VAT amount on the 'VAT revenue inflow' line in the appropriate month of form F1c or F1d below. To calculate the VAT element within your gross receipts use either of the following formula:

Gross figure $\times$ 7 $\div$ 47 = VAT element

Gross amount = £235 $\times$ 7 $\div$ 47 = £35 VAT

Net amount = £235 − £35 = £200 (Based on UK VAT rate of 17.5%)

Number 3. This is the total of your monthly revenue inflow excluding VAT.

Numbers 4, 5 and 6. Repeat the calculation above to determine the VAT element of any costs of sales payments. This figure should be transferred to the appropriate month on line 'VAT on purchase outflow' in form F1b below. The net values are entered as above.

Numbers 7, 8 and 9. Repeat the above calculation for any VATable marketing expenditure (the VAT element on other expenditure will be calculated in form F3a later on in this section).

Number 10. The total of all payments made, excluding VAT, for each month.

Number 11. Deducting 'total revenue inflow' (3) from 'total all payments made' (10) provides a monthly revenue/payments plus or minus balance, excluding VAT.

Numbers 12 and 13. The 'VAT monthly balance' figure should be taken from the VAT balance calculations on form F1c. On line 13 enter the amount to pay or reclaim. This will be the month after the VAT account transaction takes place for monthly schemes, the month after the end of your VAT quarters for most others. (If you do not need to allow for VAT payments or refunds you can ignore these two lines and transfer your answers from 11 above to 15 below in order to forecast the closing cash position at the end of each month.)

Number 15. Adding or subtracting the VAT payment/repayment figure to your monthly 'Receipts Inflow less payments' excluding VAT (11) will produce your 'total net monthly cash inflow/outflow' (15). (Do not forget, subtract VAT payments from positive balances and add them to negative balances. The opposite applies to VAT repayments.)

Number 18. The opening cash position is the cash (plus or minus) available at the start of the period. For new businesses this figure is usually zero, for most others it is the closing balance of your cash book or the remaining balance, or otherwise, of your budget for the last period.

In month 1 only add this figure to the 'total net monthly cash inflow/ outflow' (15) to produce an answer in the 'month end cash balance' (17).

Number 16. Transfer the above total to the 'balance carried forward' box (16) in month 2 and repeat the above sum. Again take the figure in the 'Month End Cash Balance' box and transfer it to the 'Balance carried forward' box in month 3, and so on.

Number 19. The figure in this last box is your forecast of the cash position at the end of the forecast period. Repeat the above calculations for each six-month period that you want to forecast.

Note: Because this cash flow forecast is using figures taken from your trading forecast, that is, sales, purchases and other overheads, the final balance may present a false picture if other non-trading income such as grants or share issue proceeds are received or expenditure on items such as dividends or corporation tax is made.

Number 14. If any unlisted items figure in your cash flow forecast, enter them as positive or negative values in the line 'other' before calculating your final monthly cash position.

F1a Monthly Forecast Sales, Costs and Profits – Months 1–6

Units

£ [   ]   Year ending [   ]

Receipts: sales and other income, cash inflow:

		Months 1–6						Total months 1–6
		1	2	3	4	5	6	
1. Revenue (VATable)	£							
2. Revenue (non VAT)	£							
3. Total Revenue Inflow (ex VAT)	£							
Payments: cash outline:								
4. Payments made (VATable)	£							
5. Payments made (non VAT)	£							
6. Total purchases outflow	£							
7. Marketing expenditure (VATable)	£							
8. Marketing expenditure (non VAT)	£							
9. Overhead expenditure	£							
10. Total payments made (ex VAT)	£							
11. Receipts inflow less payment	£							
VAT balance:								
12. VAT monthly balance	£							
13. VAT payment/refund month	£							
14. Other	£							
15. Total net monthly cash inflow/outflow	£							
16. Balance carried forward	£							
17. Month-end cash balance	£							

18. Opening cash position   £ [   ]

19. Closing balance (+ or −)

F1b   Monthly Forecast Sales, Costs and Profits – Months 7–12

Units

£ [   ]   Year ending [   ]

Receipts: sales and other income:	Total months 1–6	Months 7–12						Total months 7–12
		7	8	9	10	11	12	
1. Revenue (VATable)	£ [ ]	[ ]	[ ]	[ ]	[ ]	[ ]	[ ]	[ ]
2. Revenue (non VAT)	£ [ ]	[ ]	[ ]	[ ]	[ ]	[ ]	[ ]	[ ]
3. Total Revenue Inflow (ex VAT)	£ [ ]	[ ]	[ ]	[ ]	[ ]	[ ]	[ ]	[ ]
Payments: cash outline:								
4. Payments made (VATable)	£ [ ]	[ ]	[ ]	[ ]	[ ]	[ ]	[ ]	[ ]
5. Payments made (non VAT)	£ [ ]	[ ]	[ ]	[ ]	[ ]	[ ]	[ ]	[ ]
6. Total purchases outflow	£ [ ]	[ ]	[ ]	[ ]	[ ]	[ ]	[ ]	[ ]
7. Marketing expenditure (VATable)	£ [ ]	[ ]	[ ]	[ ]	[ ]	[ ]	[ ]	[ ]
8. Marketing expenditure (non VAT)	£ [ ]	[ ]	[ ]	[ ]	[ ]	[ ]	[ ]	[ ]
9. Overhead expenditure	£ [ ]	[ ]	[ ]	[ ]	[ ]	[ ]	[ ]	[ ]
10. Total payments made (ex VAT)	£ [ ]	[ ]	[ ]	[ ]	[ ]	[ ]	[ ]	[ ]
11. Receipts inflow less payment	£ [ ]	[ ]	[ ]	[ ]	[ ]	[ ]	[ ]	[ ]
VAT balance:								
12. VAT monthly balance	£ [ ]	[ ]	[ ]	[ ]	[ ]	[ ]	[ ]	[ ]
13. VAT payment/refund month	£ [ ]	[ ]	[ ]	[ ]	[ ]	[ ]	[ ]	[ ]
14. Other	£ [ ]	[ ]	[ ]	[ ]	[ ]	[ ]	[ ]	[ ]
15. Total net monthly cash inflow/outflow	£ [ ]	[ ]	[ ]	[ ]	[ ]	[ ]	[ ]	[ ]
16. Balance carried forward	£ [ ]	[ ]	[ ]	[ ]	[ ]	[ ]	[ ]	[ ]
17. Month-end cash balance	£ [ ]	[ ]	[ ]	[ ]	[ ]	[ ]	[ ]	[ ]

18. Closing balance (+ or –)

■ Forms F1c and F1d: VAT Balance

Calculate the VAT element of receipts and expenditure using the method shown above for form E1a. Deduct VAT on all expenditure (2) from VAT on revenue (1) and enter the result in the appropriate month of the 'VAT Balance' row. Transfer this total to VAT monthly balance (12) on form F1a above.

Repeat the calculation for the second six-month forecast.

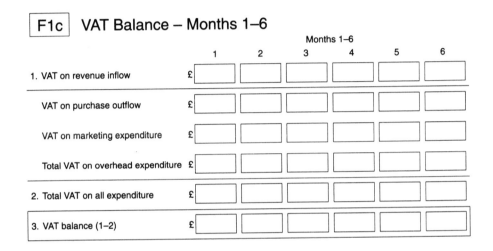

F1c   VAT Balance – Months 1–6

		Months 1–6				
	1	2	3	4	5	6
1. VAT on revenue inflow £						
VAT on purchase outflow £						
VAT on marketing expenditure £						
Total VAT on overhead expenditure £						
2. Total VAT on all expenditure £						
3. VAT balance (1–2) £						

F1d   VAT Balance – Months 7–12

		7	8	9	10	11	12
1. VAT on revenue inflow	£						
VAT on purchase outflow	£						
VAT on marketing expenditure	£						
Total VAT on overhead expenditure	£						
2. Total VAT on all expenditure	£						
3. VAT balance (1–2)	£						

■ **Cash inflow**

To help improve your cash flow forecasting you can use the following table to estimate when you are likely to receive payment for invoices issued in any month.

In the first box below, the current month, enter the percentage of each month's sales invoices that are paid in the month that they are issued. With the invoiced amounts that remain outstanding after the end of the month of issue enter the average percentage that is paid in the months following.

On form F2a use these percentages to calculate the income flow from each forecast monthly sales total on form Ea1. Use the same percentages to calculate any debtor payments from the opening debtors total from Form E2. This total should be entered in the first box on F2a.

The sum of all the monthly percentages should add up to 100 percent. If you do not offer credit terms then 100 percent would be entered in the current month box. If your customer usually retains part of the invoice amount for more than twelve months enter the average retention percentage in the twelve plus box.

Percentage sales paid in month of invoice and percentage paid in the months following

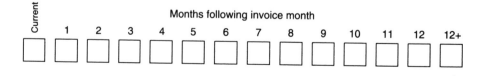

■ Form F2a: Sales Revenue and Other Income

For most businesses offering credit terms, revenue receipts are usually received over a period of time following invoicing and frequently outside the agreed trading terms. If you want to produce the most accurate forecast that you can, this form will help you.

In the table below enter the average percentage payment you expect to receive each month following invoicing. On form F2a enter your opening debtors and forecast total monthly sales. Then for each month's sales, using the above percentages, enter in the appropriate monthly box the revenue you expect to receive each month following invoicing.

Add up each of the monthly columns to obtain a total monthly revenue forecast and transfer the figures to Revenue (VATable) (1) or Revenue (non VAT) (2) on forms F1a and F1b above. Add up the 'Outstanding Balance Box' column at the end of each row to provide a forecast of debtors at the end of the period.

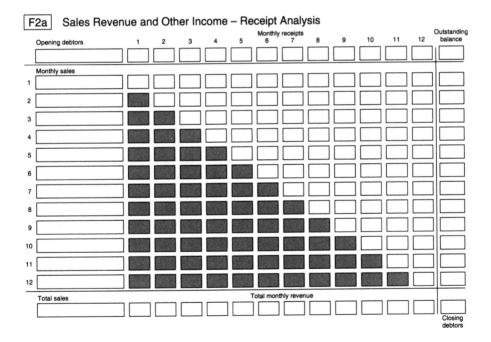

■ Cash outflow

The boxes below are completed in the same way as the cash inflow boxes. This time the aim is to help forecast the amount of cash that is likely to be paid out in any average month.

In the boxes below enter the percentage of the cost of sales purchases and marketing costs that are paid in the month they are incurred, the current month, and the percentage of these costs that are paid in the following months.

On form F2b use these percentages to calculate the payment outflow from each forecast monthly sales and marketing cost total on form Ea1. Use the same percentages to calculate any creditor payments that are to be made from the opening creditors total from form E2 that should be entered in the first box on F2a.

The sum of all the monthly percentages should add up to 100 percent. If you usually retain part of your suppliers invoice for more than twelve months enter the average retention percentage in the twelve plus box.

Percentage cost of sales and marketing costs paid in month incurred and percentage paid in the months following

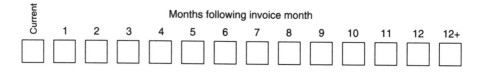

■ Form F2b: Sales, Marketing and Other Overhead Payments

Apart from the fact that this form is concerned with monthly payments rather than income it works in the same way as from F2a above. Enter your total trade and marketing creditors at the beginning of the period in the 'opening creditors' box. Enter your monthly payment forecast for this figure. List the total monthly purchases from the profit and loss forecast.

For each month calculate the percentage of these purchases that you expect to pay in succeeding months and enter the values. The total monthly payment figures should be transferred to the appropriate rows of the cash inflow/outflow forms (4) or (5) F1a and F1b after calculating the VAT element of any payments made. (VAT is calculated using the formula previously given and the resulting figures entered on the VAT balance form as before.)

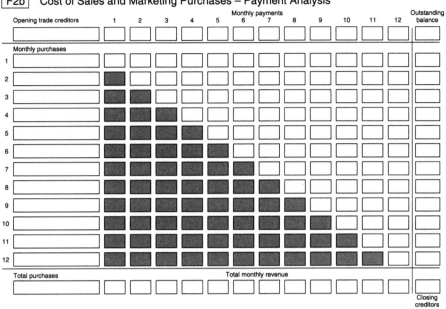

F2b   Cost of Sales and Marketing Purchases – Payment Analysis

Forms F3a and F3b: Cash Outflow – Overheads

These forms allow you to calculate your overhead payment outflow. As discussed in Chapter 14, and as with your profit and loss form D1b, you should average your outflow over the months.

Take the figures from the overhead costs on your profit and loss forecast and on forms F3a and F3b show these costs when you actually pay them – quarterly the electricity bill, rates over ten months, wages and salaries every month, and so on.

Add together the figures for VATable outflow items and calculate the VAT as before. Transfer the net amounts to overhead expenditure (9) on forms F1a and F1b and the VAT element to the Total VAT on overhead expenditure line on the VAT balance forms F1c and F1d.

F3a Cash Outflow: Overheads – Months 1–6

Enter tick if VAT rated		1	2	3	4	5	5	Total months 1–6
☐ Rent	£							
☐ Rates & water	£							
☐ Lighting & heating	£							
☐ Power	£							
☐ Repairs & maintenance	£							
☐ Insurances	£							
☐ Wages and salaries	£							
☐ Health & safety	£							
☐ Sundries	£							
☐ Office stationery	£							
☐ Office equipment	£							
☐ Telephone	£							
☐ Postage	£							
☐ Training	£							
☐ Motor expenses	£							
☐ Travel/entertainment	£							
☐ Other	£							
☐ Audit/accountancy	£							
☐ Legal fees	£							
☐ Bank charges & interest	£							
☐ Lease charges & interest	£							
☐ HP charges & interest	£							
☐ Other	£							
(A) Total passive costs – VATable	£							
(B) Total passive costs – non VAT	£							
(C) Total passive costs (A+B)	£							

F3b   Cash Outflow: Overheads – Months 7–12

£ [   ] Units

Enter tick if VAT rated

		Months 1–6	7	8	Months 7–12 9	10	11	12	Payments outstanding
☐	Rent	£							
☐	Rates & water	£							
☐	Lighting & heating	£							
☐	Power	£							
☐	Repairs & maintenance	£							
☐	Insurances	£							
☐	Wages and salaries	£							
☐	Health & safety	£							
☐	Sundries	£							
☐	Office stationery	£							
☐	Office equipment	£							
☐	Telephone	£							
☐	Postage	£							
☐	Training	£							
☐	Motor expenses	£							
☐	Travel/entertainment	£							
☐	Other	£							
☐	Audit/accountancy	£							
☐	Legal fees	£							
☐	Bank charges & interest	£							
☐	Lease charges & interest	£							
☐	HP charges & interest	£							
☐	Other	£							
(A)	Total passive costs – VATable	£							
(B)	Total passive costs – non VAT	£							
(C)	Total passive costs (A+B)	£							

Closing creditors

■ Form F4 the Action Plan

One of the last stages of the marketing planning process is to prepare a check list of everything that needs to be done to help ensure that your marketing plan is properly implemented.

As well as a list of items and activities the action plan should include time scales, budgeted costs, start and finish dates for individual items, who has been allocated to manage each task and details of any critical items or events that could disrupt the plan if not completed or available by the specified time.

For many planning purposes an action form such as this would be sufficient but where fuller project schedules are needed the information contained on this form can be used to produce a linear planning map such as a Gantt chart or critical path flow chart.

F4   The Action Plan

Items to be achieved	Time to complete	Cost (£)	Start Date	Finish date	Critical activities

Glossary of Some of the Most Commonly Used Terms in Marketing

Advertising Communications designed to sell your product or service.

AIDA An acronym for the advertising process it stands for: Attention, Interest, Decision, Action.

Brand A product recognised by its name and presentation.

Break-even point Point on a graph or table where the income or sales line crosses or exactly matches the total outgoings.

Catchment area The geographical area within which you would expect to market your products and services.

Consumers The buyers or users of your products or services.

Cost effectiveness The most efficient utilisation of capital or labour required to achieve a specific objective.

Cost plus A pricing policy for goods or services in which the selling price is determined by adding materials, labour and direct costs together and then adding a percentage profit margin to this figure. The resulting final price has been determined by the seller and not by the market place.

Gross margin The proportion of the selling price left after subtracting all directly attributable product or service costs. It is often expressed as a percentage of the selling price (see also mark-up).

Macro environment Short for macroeconomics environment. The economic conditions that prevail in the market in which you operate and influence consumers' ability to purchase.

Marketing concept The philosophy at the heart of all marketing that accepts that the needs of the customer come first.

Marketing definition The current definition of marketing is: 'Marketing is the management process reponsible for identifying, anticipating and satisfying customer requirements'.

Marketing mix Traditionally known as the four Ps but now more frequently referred to as the seven Ps. The marketing mix is the combination of all of the elements and processes within the company's control that can affect or influence the marketing of a product or service.

Marketing objectives The marketing goals you set to reach through marketing.

Marketing plan   A document encapsulating your marketing philosophy, objectives and proposed activities that is prepared prior to the start of your marketing campaign.

Marketing strategy   The overall marketing philosophy behind the marketing methods you apply in the pursuit of your marketing objectives.

Marketing tools   Techniques and methodologies regularly used in the marketing process.

Market research   The process of gathering information to evaluate the characteristics of a market or a part of it.

Market segmentation   Dividing the market into meaningful but different groups who (or which) will require a different product, service or method of communication etc.

Mark-up   The amount added to the cost of a product or service in order to arrive at the selling price. It is often expressed as a percentage of the cost price (see also gross margin).

Mission statement   The philosophy that encapsulates how the business proposes to operate.

Moving annual average   A way of deseasonalising sales by continually dividing each preceeding twelve months' sales by twelve. Over a period of time this annual average figure will adjust up or down according to the developing trend.

Premium pricing   A strategy of charging a higher than average price for your product. This will only usually be acceptable to your buyers if your product offers above-average quality or specification.

Product   The service or goods you are marketing are often referred to as the product.

Product life cycle   A theory that states that all products have a cycle of sales volume that moves through initiation to growth followed by maturity and decline.

Product perception   The image of a product and its relative place in the market as perceived by a user or potential user.

Product position   Where a business places its product in a market relative to that of its competitors. Relevant attributes include factors such as quality, value, style, price, fashion etc.

Product price   The price at which you wish to sell your goods or services. It should reflect the quality of your product relative to that of its competitors.

Product promotion   A collection of methods used to encourage the trial or purchase of a product.

Profit impact of marketing strategies (PIMS)   A model to examine the effect of marketing strategies on profitability – developed in the 1970s in the USA.

Quality assurance Processes designed to examine production quality in order to ensure that standards are maintained. There are several systems and procedures, which are recognised by awards. These include EN ISO 9000, which many UK firms are now obtaining or have obtained.

Qualitative research A market research process used to examine consumers' views on concepts and ideas in depth. The methods used may involve face-to-face interviews with individuals or semi-structured discussions with groups of people.

Quantitative research A market research process used to examine the numeric structures of markets and their constituents using statistical surveys.

Segmentation Dividing a market into smaller groupings of like-minded individuals or businesses, usually in order to improve targeting effectiveness (see targeting).

Service level strategy A written document detailing your customer service objectives and policy.

Standard industrial classification (SIC) codes An international system for classifying industrial and commercial activities by common process, for example food wholesaling, motor vehicle manufacture. There have been regular revisions to the system. The latest European revisions were made in 1992.

Strategic objectives What a business wants to achieve during a specific time period. Usually, medium- to long-term strategic objectives need to be quantified and realistic.

SWOT analysis The process of examining your products, services or the complete business. SWOT stands for Strengths, Weaknesses, Opportunities and Threats.

Target market The potential consumers of your product. They may be young people, or females or electronics manufacturers. Certainly not everybody will wish or be able to buy your products, so accurate targeting avoids marketing to those unlikely to purchase (see also segmentation).

Targeting Focusing your marketing effort on a segment or segments of the market to improve consumer response, for example childrens clothes are targeted at families with children.

Vision statement Usually expressed as an unquantified objective, the vision statement is what the business or organisation *wishes to do* and is often confused with the mission statement – the way the business or organisation *proposes to operate* – and the strategic objective – what it *expects to achieve*.

Index